LEARN 14 CHC
FOR (
Daily Lessons for Songwriters and Guitarsists of All Levels!
By Troy Nelson

MW01485868

To download the companion audio files for this book, visit: www.troynelsonmusic.com/download/chordprogressions

ISBN 9781797588605   Copyright © 2019 Troy Nelson
International Copyright Secured. All Rights Reserved

INTRODUCTION

As guitarists, we spend a lot of our practice time running through scales and learning how to use them over chord progressions. Lead guitar gets all the glory, after all. But how well do you understand those chords you're playing over? Do you know how those chords are constructed, or why one chord was chosen over another?

Or maybe you're stuck in a rut, playing the same chord progressions you learned from your guitar teacher or your favorite songs, never knowing which way to turn to find harmonic inspiration. If any of these scenarios describes you, don't worry—you're not alone. Every developing guitarist, at one point or another, encounters the same problems. The fact that you're reading this book says a lot about your guitar aspirations.

Learn 14 Chord Progressions for Guitar in 14 Days seems pretty self-explanatory, but there's so much more to it than just learning how to play several new chord progressions. After starting with some basic chord theory so you'll understand the concepts that you'll encounter along the way, the book quickly introduces the first of 14 chord progressions—all of which are presented as short music exercises, in various keys and styles, and using several different chord voicings and guitar techniques. So, in addition to learning new progressions, you'll increase your chord vocabulary, learn several guitar techniques and styles, and, in turn, become a more well-rounded guitarist and musician. While the book might be a bit too advanced for absolute beginners, guitarists at the "late beginner" or "early intermediate" stage in their development should find most of the material quite manageable.

Learn 14 Chord Progressions for Guitar in 14 Days is divided into 14 lessons, one for each day of the two-week program. Within each lesson/day are six sections: Open-Chord Strumming, Open-Chord Arpeggios, Open-Chord Fingerpicking, Barre Chords, Extended Chords, and 6/8 Meter. The goal is to spend 15 minutes practicing the music exercises in each section, for a total of 90 minutes (15 X 6 = 90) per day. Week 1 introduces seven popular major-key chord progressions, while Week 2 presents seven minor progressions.

OPEN-CHORD STRUMMING
Each day starts with relatively easy open-chord strumming to get you acquainted with the sound of that day's progression. The chord changes are presented in the key of C (A minor in Week 2) and the rhythms get progressively more challenging as the book unfolds. As with all of the music examples in the book, the progression is presented in tab, with chord diagrams accompanying the changes so you can quickly visualization the chord shapes and determine the best way to voice (finger) them.

OPEN-CHORD ARPEGGIOS
The next 15 minutes of the practice session are devoted to arpeggios (notes of chords picked individually rather than strummed). Arpeggios are a popular rhythm-guitar style, so it's important to learn how to play progressions in this style. Like the strumming section, the arpeggios get more challenging as the book progresses. In an effort to get your ears acquainted with hearing progressions in other keys, this section transposes the day's chord changes to the key of G major (E minor in Week 2).

OPEN-CHORD FINGERPICKING

At the 30-minute mark, the progression moves to the key of A (F# minor in Week 2) and the focus shifts to fingerpicking—another important rhythm-guitar technique. The emphasis here is on the thumb (*p*), index (*i*), middle (*m*), and ring (*a*) fingers, which are used to arpeggiate the chords of each day's progression. Like the other sections, the music examples get a bit more complex as you progress through the book.

BARRE CHORDS

After 45 minutes of playing open chords, this section focuses on performing each day's progression exclusively with barre chords. For those who are unfamiliar with barre chords, Days 1 and 2 ease into these shapes by starting with two- and three-note power chords (i.e., pared-down barre chords) before diving into full-blown five- and six-string barre-chord shapes on subsequent days. F major (Week 1) and D minor (Week 2) are the featured keys in this section.

EXTENDED CHORDS

After spending an hour with relatively simple major and minor triads, the Extended Chords section is an opportunity to hear each day's progression played with a more sophisticated set of chords, everything from major and minor sevenths to dominant 9ths and 13ths, among others. These "extended" chords are not only more difficult to voice, they can make hearing the changes a bit more challenging, too, so this section provides a good opportunity to work on ear training, as well. The main genres featured here are jazz and funk, and we encounter our first "flat" key, Bb (G minor in Week 2).

6/8 METER

After focusing on chords and technique for the majority of the lesson, playing everything in 4/4 meter, this section introduces a new time signature, 6/8. If you're unfamiliar with this meter, 6/8 has a waltz feel similar to 3/4, but you'll hear the former much more frequently in popular music than the latter, so it's important to familiarize yourself it. Day 1 starts with basic open chords in the key of D (B minor in Week 2), which are strummed in a straight eighth-note rhythm to get you acquainted with the basic feel of the meter. In subsequent days, the rhythms and technical aspects of the music get progressively more challenging.

HOW TO USE THIS BOOK

Granted, 90 minutes of practice per day can seem daunting, especially if you're unaccustomed to sessions lasting longer than 20–30 minutes. And that's OK! Just because the book is structured to teach you 14 chord progressions in 14 days doesn't mean you have to follow the program precisely. On the contrary, if you have, say, 30 minutes to devote to the book each day, then simply extend each lesson (day) to a three-day practice session. The material is there for you to use, whether you get through the book in 14 days or 40.

While the 14-day plan is the goal, it's probably unrealistic for some. The important thing is to stick with it because the material in this book will have you playing new chord progressions fluently and confidently, and in several different styles. How quickly just depends on the amount of time you're able to spend on getting there.

Before you begin your daily sessions, however, I suggest spending 10–15 minutes listening to the accompanying audio to get a feel for the forthcoming exercises, as well as reading through each section's introductory material to better understand what you're about to learn. That way, you can spend the *full* 90 minutes (or however much time you have to practice that day) playing the music examples.

To help keep you on track in your practice sessions, time codes are included throughout the book. Simply set the timer on your smart phone to 90 minutes (1:30) and move on to a new section every 15 minutes. Or, you can set the timer to 15 minutes (0:15) and move on to the next section when the timer goes off.

Next, set your metronome (or click track or drum loop) to a tempo at which you can play the exercise all the way through without making too many mistakes (40–50 beats per minute is probably a good starting point for most exercises). Once you're able to play the exercise cleanly, increase your tempo by 4–5 BPM. Again, make sure you can play through the exercise without making too many mistakes. If the speed is too fast, back off a bit until your execution is precise. Continue to increase your tempo incrementally until it's time to move on to the next section.

There will be times when the timer goes off and you feel like you didn't adequately learn the material. When this happens, I suggest moving on to the next section nonetheless. It may seem counterintuitive, but it's better to continue progressing through the book than to extend the practice time in order to perfect the material. After you've completed the book, you can always go back and review the exercises. In fact, I recommend it. Making steady progress, while not always perfectly, keeps you mentally sharp and motived. Focusing too much on any one exercise is a sure way to sidetrack your sessions.

Lastly—and this is important—if you ever feel yourself getting physically fatigued or pain develops in any part of your body, especially your hands or arms, immediately take a break until the discomfort subsides, whether it's for 10 minutes, an hour, or for the rest of the day. You never want to push yourself beyond your physical limits and cause permanent damage. As mentioned earlier, the material isn't going anywhere; you can always go back to it when you're feeling 100%.

THEORY BEHIND CHORD PROGRESSIONS

In order to better understand the material that follows, a short tutorial on chord theory is in order. *Chord theory* is simply theory that is focused on the harmonic aspects of music, as opposed to the melodic ones. For the sake of efficiency, we're going to limit this discussion to two components of chord theory: chord construction and chord progressions.

Chord construction is the study of how scale tones are combined to form various chords, from basic triads and seventh chords to more sophisticated harmonies (Cmaj9, Am11, G13, etc.).

A *chord progression* is the order in which various chords are arranged relative to the music's root, or tonic. If all of the chords in the progression come from the same scale, or key, the progression is considered to be *diatonic*. Conversely, if one or more chords fall outside the scale, the progression is *non-diatonic*. Although both types are found in all styles of music, diatonic progressions are far and away the most common. In this book, 10 of the progressions we'll study are of the diatonic variety, while the other four are non-diatonic (two major and two minor).

CHORD CONSTRUCTION

Chord construction involves stacking scale tones to form relative triads or seventh chords, and even extended chords like ninths, 11ths, and 13ths. In this book, we're going to mostly stick to major and minor triads and seventh chords, with a few others occasionally thrown into the mix.

Triads

The most fundamental of all chords is the triad. A *triad* is a three-note chord that can be major, minor, augmented, or diminished in quality. The triads that you'll most frequently encounter—in this book and elsewhere—are major and minor.

The foundation of Western music, the *major scale* is a seven-note scale that is comprised of a specific series of whole steps (distance of two frets) and half steps (one fret):

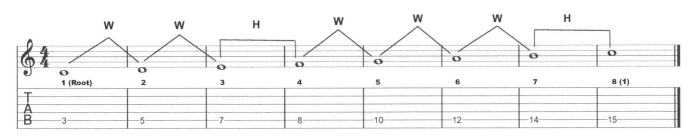

As you can see, the C major scale contains no sharps or flats, and half steps naturally occur between the notes E and F, as well as between B and C. You can apply this intervallic formula (whole–whole–half–whole–whole–whole–half) to any of the 12 notes of the musical alphabet to get its corresponding major scale:

SCALE DEGREE:	1	2	3	4	5	6	7	8 (1)
C MAJOR	C	D	E	F	G	A	B	C
G MAJOR	G	A	B	C	D	E	F#	G
D MAJOR	D	E	F#	G	A	B	C#	D
A MAJOR	A	B	C#	D	E	F#	G#	A
E MAJOR	E	F#	G#	A	B	C#	D#	E
B MAJOR	B	C#	D#	E	F#	G#	A#	B
F#/Gb MAJOR	F#/Gb	G#/Ab	A#/Bb	B/Cb	C#/Db	D#/Eb	E#/F	F#/Gb
C#/Db MAJOR	C#/Db	D#/Eb	E#/F	F#/Gb	G#/Ab	A#/Bb	B#/C	C#/Db
Ab MAJOR	Ab	Bb	C	Db	Eb	F	G	Ab
Eb MAJOR	Eb	F	G	Ab	Bb	C	D	Eb
Bb MAJOR	Bb	C	D	Eb	F	G	A	Bb
F MAJOR	F	G	A	Bb	C	D	E	F

A major triad (1–3–5) is built from the root, 3rd, and 5th of its relative major scale. This holds true for any key. Below are major triads constructed from a few of the major scales listed above:

6

Like the major scale, the *minor scale* is comprised of seven notes. In fact, the minor scale (a.k.a. the natural minor scale or Aeolian mode) is the *relative minor* of the major scale, meaning both scales contain the *same* notes. For example, the relative minor of C major (C–D–E–F–G–A–B) is A minor (A–B–C–D–E–F–G). If you were to play the C major scale but starting and ending on its sixth note, A, you would be playing the A *minor* scale. The only difference between the two scales are their starting points, but that difference is stark, sonically.

The same principle applies to each of the 12 major scales. For example, to find the relative minor of G major, we simply count up the scale until we reach the sixth degree: G (1), A (2), B (3), C (4), D (5), E (6). What we discover is that E minor (E–F#–G–A–B–C–D) is the relative minor of G major. Both scales contain the exact same notes; the only difference is their starting points (and the sound!). Here's a table containing all 12 minor scales:

SCALE DEGREE:	1	2	3	4	5	6	7	8 (1)
A MINOR	A	B	C	D	E	F	G	A
E MINOR	E	F#	G	A	B	C	D	E
B MINOR	B	C#	D	E	F#	G	A	B
F# MINOR	F#	G#	A	B	C#	D	E	F#
C# MINOR	C#	D#	E	F#	G#	A	B	C#
G# MINOR	G#	A#	B	C#	D#	E	F#	G#
D#/Eb MINOR	D#/Eb	E#/F	F#/Gb	G#/Ab	A#/Bb	B/Cb	C#/Db	D#/Eb
A#/Bb MINOR	A#/Bb	B#/C	C#/Db	D#/Eb	E#/F	F#/Gb	G#/Ab	A#/Bb
F MINOR	F	G	Ab	Bb	C	Db	Eb	F
C MINOR	C	D	Eb	F	G	Ab	Bb	C
G MINOR	G	A	Bb	C	D	Eb	F	G
D MINOR	D	E	F	G	A	Bb	C	D

A minor triad (1–b3–5) is built from the root, b3rd, and 5th of its relative minor scale (you can also think of it as a major triad with a lowered 3rd). This holds true for any key. The next example features minor triads constructed from a few of the minor scales listed above:

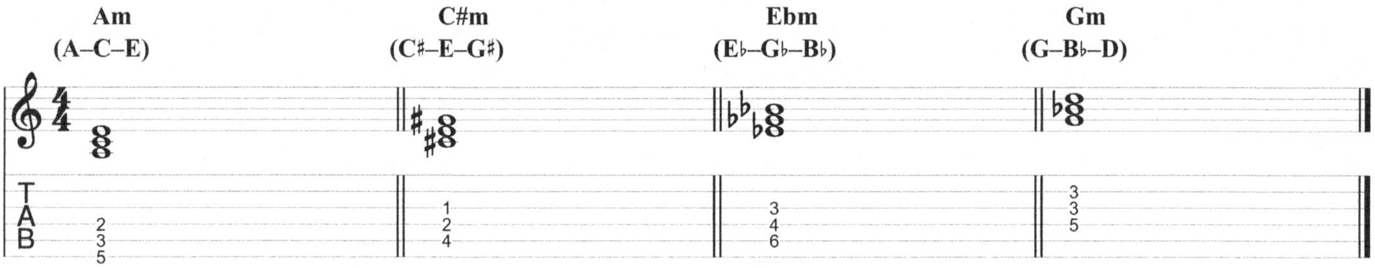

Am
(A–C–E)

C#m
(C#–E–G#)

Ebm
(Eb–Gb–Bb)

Gm
(G–Bb–D)

The other two triads, augmented (1–3–#5) and diminished (1–b3–b5), can be thought of as alterations of the major and minor triads, respectively. To form an augmented triad, simply raise (i.e., augment) a major triad's 5th one half step; likewise, to achieve a diminished triad, simply *lower* (diminish) a minor triad's 5th one half step.

C
(C–E–G)

Caug
(C–E–G#)

Cm
(C–Eb–G)

Cdim
(C–Eb–Gb)

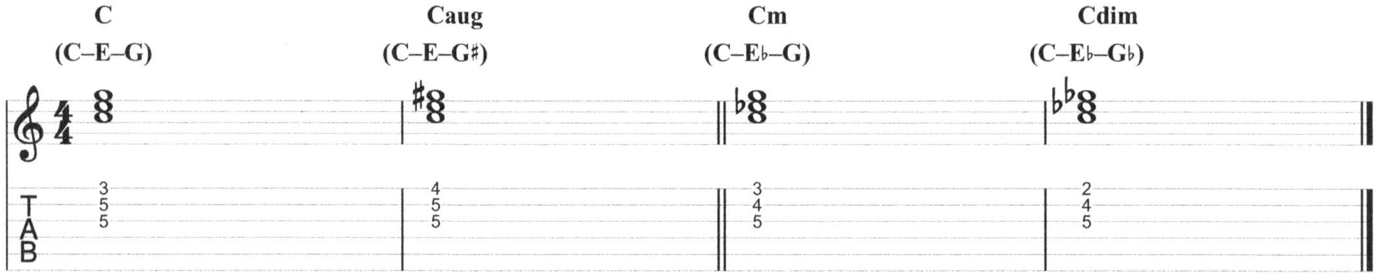

Seventh Chords

Although not quite as popular as triads, seventh chords are found in practically every musical setting, from jazz and blues to country and pop. Like triads, seventh chords come in several qualities, with major, minor, and dominant being the most popular; unlike triads, however, seventh chords are comprised of *four* notes. Major seventh (1–3–5–7), minor seventh (1–b3–5–b7), and dominant seventh (1–3–5–b7) chords are built from the root, 3rd, 5th and 7th of their relative major, minor, and dominant (Mixolydian) scales, respectively.

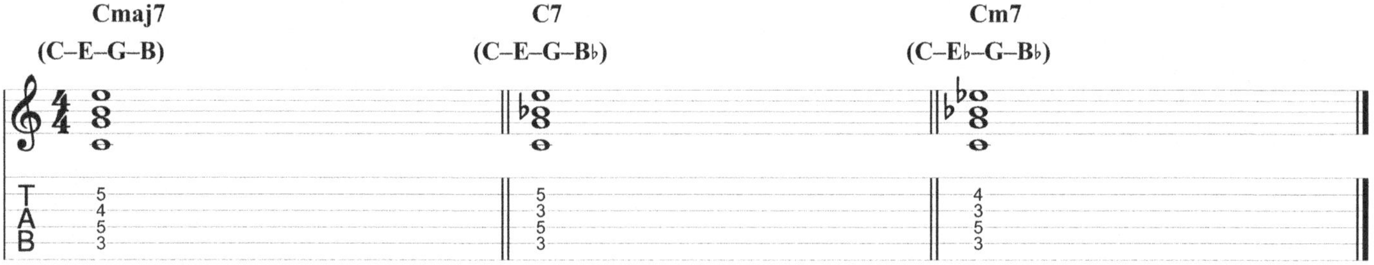

Cmaj7
(C–E–G–B)

C7
(C–E–G–Bb)

Cm7
(C–Eb–G–Bb)

As you can see, by simply lowering by a half step (one fret) the 7th of the Cmaj7 chord, the chord becomes dominant in quality (C7). The distinguishing characteristic of a dominant seventh chord is the presence of both a major (3rd) and minor (b7th) chord tone. This major/minor juxtaposition in what gives the blues its distinct, melancholy sound—and why so many dominant seventh chords are used in that music.

The minor seventh chord also has a b7th. But what differentiates it from the dominant seventh chord is the presence of a *minor* 3rd, as well.

Extended Chords

Any note that is stacked on top of the 7th is considered an extension. The *extended chord* family includes 9ths, 11ths, and 13ths, and like seventh chords, extended chords can be major, minor, or dominant in quality.

A 9th chord is a seventh chord with a major 9th interval (a major 2nd interval voiced an octave higher) stacked on top. An 11th chord is a ninth chord with a perfect 11th (a perfect 4th interval voiced an octave higher) on top. And a 13th chord is an 11th chord with a major 13th (a major 6th interval voiced an octave higher) on top.

Because guitar players are limited to four or five fingers when voicing a chord, it's general practice to eliminate certain pitches from extended chords. Typically, the first pitch to be jettisoned is the 5th, as it plays no part in defining the chord's quality (major, minor, or dominant), nor is it an extension. The next chord tones to go are typically extensions below the one that defines the chord. For example, if you were to play a C13 chord (1–3–5–b7–9–11–13: C–E–G–Bb–D–F–A), you could eliminate the 9th and 11th and still maintain the integrity of the chord because the major 3rd (E), minor 7th (Bb), and 13th (A) are still present, which give the chord its dominant 13th sound. Moreover, if you are playing with a bass player and he is holding down the root, you could eliminate the tonic (C) from the chord, too.

Below are a few common extended chords, all voiced in the key of C.

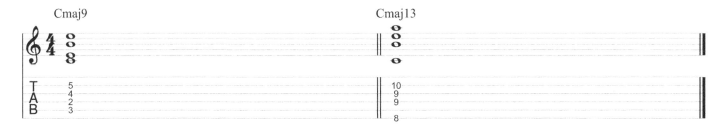

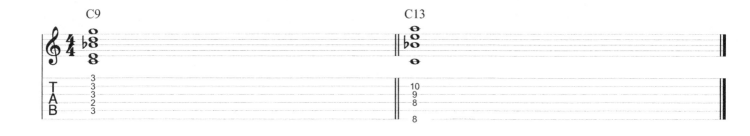

CHORD PROGRESSIONS

A *chord progression* is a series of chords with a specific tonality, or sound, relative to the tonic chord. When all of the chords belong to the same major or minor key, the progression is considered to be *diatonic*. If one or more chords fall outside the key, then the progression is considered to be *non-diatonic*.

Diatonic progressions are prevalent in popular music, and pop songs that *do* employ non-diatonic progressions usually feature only one or two chords that fall outside the key. The best genre for hearing non-diatonic progressions in action is jazz, which typically involves highly sophisticated non-diatonic chord changes. In this book, we'll focus on both diatonic and non-diatonic chord progressions, with an emphasis on the former.

If we take the C major scale and build diatonic triads on top of each scale degree, we end up with the following chords:

Notice that none of the triads contains a sharp or flat—they're all "natural" notes—which is an indication that all of the chords are relative to the key of C major (or A minor). If you refer back to our table containing the 12 major scales, you can see how some of these triads must be altered (relative to their parallel major scale) to accommodate the "new" key—in this case, C major. For example, the D major scale (D–E–F#–G–A–B–C#) contains a major 3rd, F#, but the ii chord in C major, Dm, is minor in quality. The solution is to lower the 3rd from F# to F (one half step) to accommodate the C major key center. The same goes for the iii chord: the 3rd of the E major scale (E–F#–G#–A–B–C#–D#) is G#, which must be lowered one half step (to G) to make it minor in quality and diatonic to C major. Some of the triads, like F and G major, require no adjustments at all.

This type of analysis (i.e., comparing each triad to its parallel major scale) can be a bit confusing. What's important to know is that, regardless of the key, the chord (triad) qualities in a diatonic progression always remain the same: I–ii–iii–IV–V–vi–viidim (major–minor–minor–major–major–minor–diminished). We're simply taking the notes of a major scale and stacking 3rds (every other note of the scale) on top of them. The result is the seven triads illustrated in the previous music example.

The Roman numerals indicate the scale degree relative to the tonic, as well as whether the triad is major (uppercase) or minor (lowercase). (Diminished triads are also represented by a lowercase Roman numeral, plus the abbreviation "dim" or a small, circular symbol.) The Roman-numeral system is extremely helpful in regard to transposing progressions to other keys—as long as you have a firm grasp of the 12 major keys!

The same concept applies to diatonic triads in minor keys. Here are the seven triads that are built from the A minor scale:

If you look closely, you'll notice that the chords in A minor are exactly the same as the chords in C major, only in a different order: i–iidim–III–iv–v–VI–VII (Am–Bdim–C–Dm–Em–F–G). Despite the different sequence, three of the triads are minor, three are major, and one is diminished—just like the triads of the C major scale! (**Note:** You will sometimes see the minor-scale Roman numerals written to reflect the *parallel* major key rather than the *relative* key. In the case of A minor, the Roman-numerals would reflect the A major scale [A–B–C#–D–E–F#–G#]: i– iidim–bIII–iv–v–bVI–bVII.)

The same concept applies to seventh (and extended) chords. Here are the seven diatonic seventh chords that can be built from the notes of the C major scale:

And, just so we're thorough, here are the seven diatonic seventh chords in the key of A minor:

Again, the chords in both keys are exactly the same, only the sequence is different. By stacking one more 3rd on top of the triads of the two scales, we get two major seventh chords (Cmaj7 and Fmaj7), three minor seventh chords (Dm7, Em7, and Am7), one dominant seventh chord (G7), and one minor seventh flat-five chord (Bm7b5). The sequences and chord qualities remain constant in any major or minor key.

WEEK 1: MAJOR PROGRESSIONS

DAY 1: I–IV PROGRESSION

Our first progression, I–IV, is heard in popular music perhaps more than any other, whether it's a simple two-chord sequence like the one we'll study here, or as part of a larger three- or four-chord progression (which we'll cover in a bit). The strong appeal of moving from the I (tonic) chord to the IV (sub-dominant) chord, or vice versa, is only surpassed by one other two-chord change, I to V (dominant). Moving from I to IV is the common change in the first few bars of a standard 12-bar blues progression, but it's also found in practically every genre of music (see list below).

EXAMPLES IN POPULAR SONGS:
"Born in the U.S.A." by Bruce Springsteen (Key of B)
"Boys 'Round Here" by Blake Shelton (Key of A)
"Ring of Fire" by Johnny Cash (Key of G)
"What I Got" by Sublime (Key of D)

OPEN-CHORD STRUMMING (1:30–1:15)

Our first example features the I–IV progression in the key of C. The rhythm is pretty straightforward: quarter notes are strummed on beats 1 and 3 and eighth notes occupy beats 2 and 4, giving it a country/folk sound. Meanwhile, the chords are common open-position C and F voicings.

When switching from C to F, leave you index finger in place (fret 1, string 2) while shifting your ring and middle fingers from strings 5–4 to strings 4–3. You will, however, need to slightly adjust your index finger in order to barre strings 2–1 for the F chord.

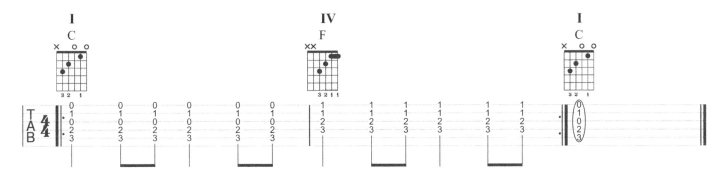

OPEN-CHORD ARPEGGIOS (1:15–1:00)

Here, the I–IV progression is performed in the key of G. Common G (I) and C (IV) chords (we used the latter chord in the previous section) are arpeggiated in open position, using a pattern that ascends the chord/strings until reaching the high E string (beat 3), where it reverses course and descends the strings. Be sure to let the notes of the chords ring out fully.

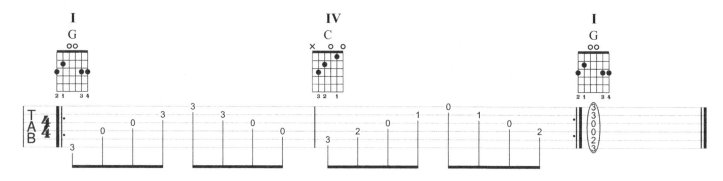

OPEN-CHORD FINGERPICKING (1:00–0:45)

Our next example involves fingerpicking the I–IV progression, which is performed here in the key of A. Open A (I) and D (IV) chords are arpeggiated in a steady eighth-note rhythm, with the thumb plucking string 5 (A chord) and string 4 (D chord) on every downbeat. The spaces (upbeats), meanwhile, are filled by alternating notes plucked with the index (string 3) and middle (string 2) fingers, with the ring finger catching the final note of each measure (string 1).

If you're new to fingerpicking, this example will be a bit challenging at first, so take it slow and concentrate on using the correct finger for each note. One way to approach this pattern is to start with just the thumb, plucking strings 5–4 in a steady quarter-note rhythm—without involving the other fingers. Once you're comfortable with the thumb, start to introduce the other fingers to the pattern, one note at a time.

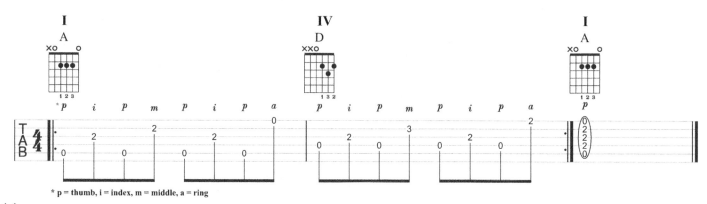

14

BARRE CHORDS (0:45–0:30)

As you may have noticed, this first barre-chord examples doesn't contain barre chords at all, and that's on purpose because, for most people, barre chords are difficult to grasp (pardon the pun) at first. Therefore, we're going to begin our barre-chord studies with two-note *power chords*, which are stripped-down version of the former, containing only the root and 5th of the chord (because they lack a 3rd, they are neither major nor minor). Power chords are a favorite among rock and metal guitarist, but you'll often hear them in other genres, as well.

This example performs the I–IV progression in the key of F. Both chords—F5 (I) and Bb5 (IV)—are voiced in first position, so making the change simply involves shifting the voicing up one string pair. The rhythm here is the same as the one used in our very first example (C to F), with quarter notes occupying beats 1 and 3, and eight notes appearing on beats 2 and 4. "P.M." indicates those notes should be palm muted, meaning your pick-hand palm should be resting on the string while it's struck.

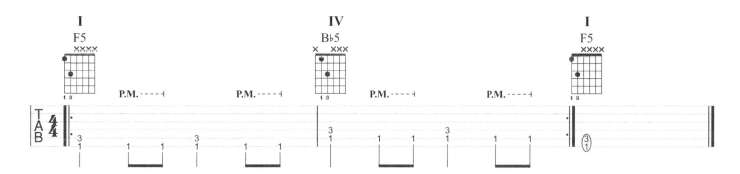

EXTENDED CHORDS (0:30–0:15)

In this section, we're going to tackle our first "flat" key, Bb, which will turn our I–IV progression into Bb–Eb. Instead of using basic triads, we're going to play the changes with a common major seventh voicing. So, once you're comfortable with the Bbmaj7 chord, simply slide your hand up five frets, playing the same voicing at fret 6, which now makes it Ebmaj7.

Notice the dots above each of the quarter notes. These are *staccato markings*, which mean the quarter notes should be played short, or clipped, rather than allowed to ring out for the full beat. Listen to the audio demonstration to hear these in action.

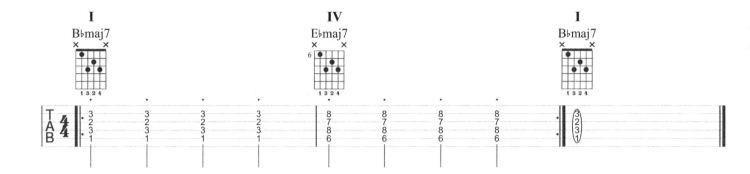

6/8 METER (0:15–0:00)

If 6/8 meter is new to you, here's what it entails: the "6" means each measure contains six beats, and the "8" indicates that eighth notes are equivalent to one beat (4 = quarter note, 8 = eighth notes, etc.).

In the example below—a I–IV progression in the key of D (D–G), played with standard open triads—eighth notes are used exclusively. You can count this meter thusly: "*One*, two, three, *four*, five, six," etc. You can also think of 6/8 in terms of 4/4 time, with eighth-note triplets occupying each beat. For this, tap your foot in a quarter-note pulse while counting, "One-trip-let, two-trip-let," etc.

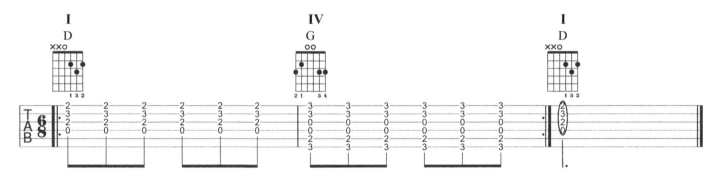

16

Today, we're going to introduce the V chord, the "other" major chord created by harmonizing the major scale, to the chord changes from yesterday, I–IV. Instead of just tacking the V chord onto the end of the progression (which is perfectly acceptable!), we're going to split the I and IV chords to create a I–V–IV progression. Of course, this is just one of several ways these three chords can be arranged, but it's a good starting point. Be sure to check out some of the songs listed below to hear how the progression can be used as the foundation for sections—or even entire songs.

EXAMPLES IN POPULAR SONGS:
"All the Small Things" by Blink-182 (Key of C)
"Baba O'Riley" by The Who (Key of F)
"Bad Moon Rising" by Creedence Clearwater Revival (Key of D)
"Knockin' on Heaven's Door" by Guns N' Roses (Key of G)

OPEN-CHORD STRUMMING (1:30–1:15)

Like yesterday's open-chord strumming, this example is played in the key of C. Be sure to look closely at the fingering suggestion for the G chord. Using the ring finger on string 6 makes the chord changes much more efficient. As for strumming, you can perform the figure with downstrokes exclusively or with continuous alternate strumming, using downstrokes on each downbeat, and upstrokes on the upbeats.

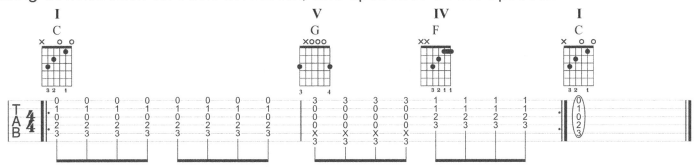

OPEN-CHORD ARPEGGIOS (1:15–1:00)

This example, played in the key of G, is similar to the progression in the previous section in that the I chord (in this case, G) is played for an entire measure and the V (D) and IV (C) chords each occupy just two beats. After an ascending/descending pattern in measure 1, the V and IV chords are articulated with four-note ascending patterns. As with all of the arpeggio examples in this book, be sure to let the notes of the chords ring out to their fullest potential.

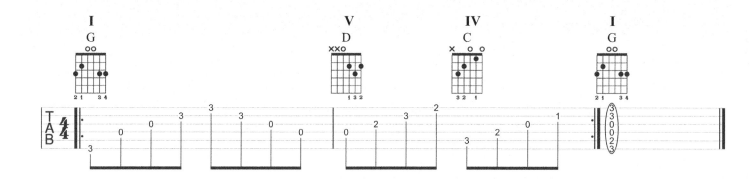

OPEN-CHORD FINGERPICKING (1:00–0:45)

In this next example, all three chords of today's progression (I, V, and IV) are played for a full measure, using a fingerpicking pattern that consists of the thumb hitting each chord's root in a quarter-note rhythm while the ring, middle, and index fingers alternate (a–m–i–m) on the upbeats. We're in the key of A here, so A is the tonic, E is the V chord, and D is the IV.

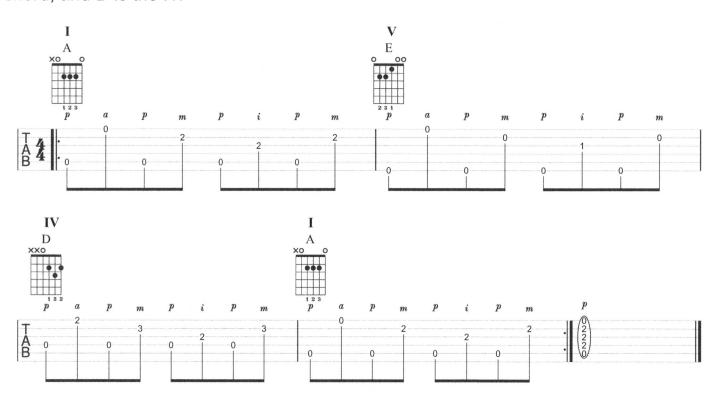

BARRE CHORDS (0:45–0:30)

In preparation for the fully-fretted barre chords that we'll eventually encounter, the figure below expands on yesterday's power-chord exercise by introducing the octave, thereby turning the chords into three-note voicings. Palm mutes are present once again, as well, but this time a gallop rhythm is used in place of straight eighth notes. Use a down-down-up picking pattern for these gallops.

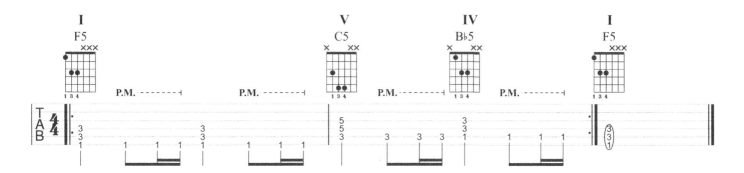

EXTENDED CHORDS (0:30–0:15)

If you recall our discussion on extended chords in the book's introduction, you'll remember that, when harmonizing the major scale with seventh chords, the V chord is dominant (V7). Therefore, when the V chord arrives in the exercise below, we must adjust our fingering from a major seventh voicing (Bbmaj7) to a dominant seventh one (F7). Fortunately, this only requires the middle finger to be lifted from string 3. Then, to play the IV chord, Ebmaj7, the middle finger is simply returned to the same string.

6/8 METER (0:15–0:00)

Rhythmically, we're going to up the ante a bit in this next exercise. Instead of the straight eighths from yesterday, this example features 16th notes on the second beat of each three-note grouping. Strum these groupings with a down/down-up/down pattern. This means that you'll strum downward on each eighth note (beat), and upstrum only on the second 16th note of each 16th-note pair.

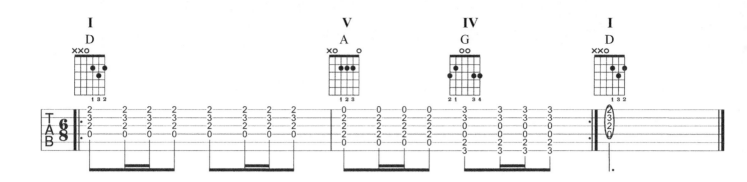

Today, we're going to explore our first four-chord progression, I–vi–ii–V. As you've probably figured out by now, progressions come in varying lengths, but perhaps none more popular than the four-chord variety—there's just something special about the symmetry and sound of playing four different chords over the course of two, four, or even eight bars.

This progression also includes another "first" for us: the inclusion of not only one, but two minor chords, vi and ii. The vi chord, or relative minor, is by far the most prevalent minor chord in major-key progressions, with the ii chord coming in second, albeit a distant second. The ii–V sequence is found all over jazz music, but is less common in pop and rock. Nevertheless, the I–vi–ii–V progression was frequently heard on the radio in the '50s and '60s, and, with a resurgence in retro sounds in pop music lately, we'll no doubt hear more of it again soon.

EXAMPLES IN POPULAR SONGS:
"Back to You" by John Mayer (Key of A)
"Hungry Heart" by Bruce Springsteen (Key of C#)
"Return to Sender" by Elvis Presley (Key of Eb)
"We Belong Together" by Ritchie Valens (Key of F)

OPEN-CHORD STRUMMING (1:30–1:15)

When performed in the key of C, the I–vi–ii–V progression becomes C–Am–Dm–G. When using open triads like our example here, the C to Am change only requires relocating the ring finger from fret 3 of string 5 to fret 2 of string 3. Also, although requiring all three fingers to shift to new strings, the Am and Dm shapes are similar, which makes relocation less difficult. Finally, the progression is capped by a big ol' G chord. The Dm–G change is probably the trickiest, but here's a tip: leave your ring finger planted on fret 3 of string 2 as you make the change, using it as a pivot point instead of lifting all of your fingers from the fretboard.

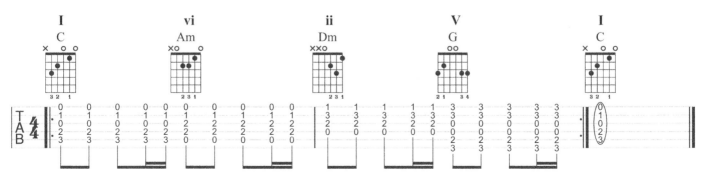

OPEN-CHORD ARPEGGIOS (1:15–1:00)

Our arpeggio exercise today is played in the key of G and involves a pattern that mostly descends the voicings. For each chord, pluck the low root note with a downstroke, then use one continuous upstroke for the remaining three notes of the chord. Use this pattern throughout.

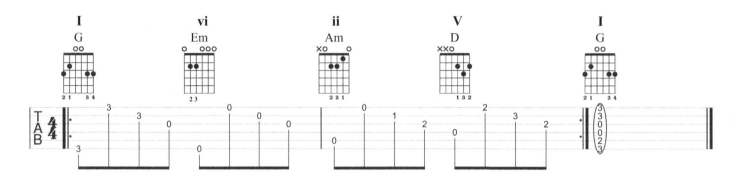

OPEN-CHORD FINGERPICKING (1:00–0:45)

On Days 1 and 2, we laid the groundwork for what we're going to explore today: Travis picking. *Travis picking* is a fingerpicking technique made famous by country artist Merle Travis and involves plucking alternating bass notes with the thumb while simultaneously plucking melody notes on the treble strings with the other fingers.

In the example below, the I–vi–ii–V progression is played in the key of A and features a Travis-picking pattern consisting of a thumb-and-middle-finger "pinch" on the first beat of each chord, followed by thumb alternations on the bass strings. The biggest challenge with this exercise is keeping a steady pulse with the thumb, so be sure to practice with a metronome or drum loop—really, anything that can keep time.

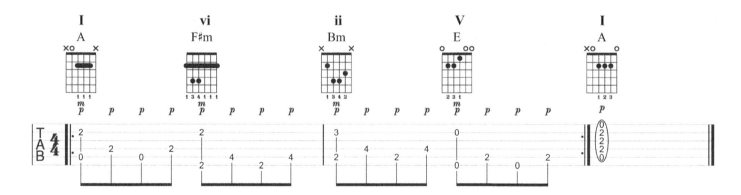

BARRE CHORDS (0:45–0:30)

After a couple of days of playing power chords, now we're ready to tackle fully-fretted barre chords. In the exercise below, the I–vi–ii–V progression is performed in the key of F, using six-string major (F and C) and minor (Dm and Gm) voicings. Fortunately, changing between the two types only requires lifting the middle finger from the third string.

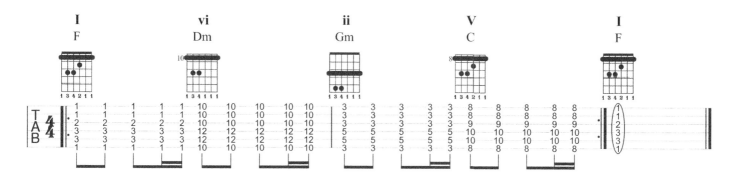

EXTENDED CHORDS (0:30–0:15)

Now that we have some barre chords under our belt, let's apply the same concept to extended chords. The jazzy example below features the I–vi–ii–V progression in the key of Bb, played with a handful of major, minor, and dominant seventh barre chords.

The first chord, Bbmaj7, should look familiar because it's the same voicing we used on Days 1 and 2, only an index-finger barre is used to incorporate string 1, as well. Meanwhile, the Gm7 and F7 voicings are variations of the six-string barre-chords we just learned, so they should seem somewhat familiar. The Cm7 chord, however, is a new one for us, but a good one to know because it's probably the most commonly used voicing for a minor seventh chord among guitarists. So, get to know this one intimately.

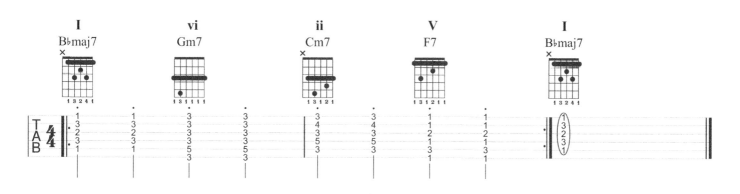

6/8 METER (0:15–0:00)

Rhythmically, this exercise is a continuation of the 6/8 examples from Days 1 and 2. On Day 1, we started with straight eighth notes. Then, on Day 2, we added 16th notes to the middle beat of each three-note grouping. Now, we're going to extend the 16th-note rhythm to beats 3 and 6 of each measure. So, each three-beat grouping now consists of an eighth note and four consecutive 16th notes. Listen to the accompanying audio to hear how the strumming should sound.

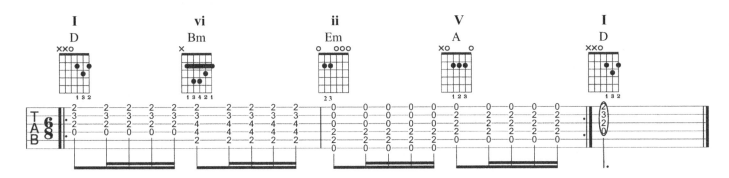

DAY 4: I–iii–vi–IV PROGRESSION

Of the three minor chords created by harmonizing the major scale (ii, iii, and vi), the iii chord gets the least action. But that's not to say you won't hear it on the radio. On the contrary, the iii chord makes frequent appearances on pop stations (see the list below), as well as country radio. When preceded by the I (tonic) chord, the iii chord lends the progression a distinctly moody feel.

Today, we're going to explore the I–iii–vi–IV progression so we can hear this change firsthand. In addition to the I and iii chords, this set of changes also involves the relative minor (vi) and sub-dominant (IV) chords.

EXAMPLES IN POPULAR SONGS:
"Price Tag" by Jessie J (Key of F)
"Secrets" by OneRepublic (Key of D)
"Someone Like You" by Adele (Key of A)
"So What" by Pink (Key of A)
"We Can't Stop" by Miley Cyrus (Key of E)

OPEN-CHORD STRUMMING (1:30–1:15)

Our strumming example today involves a predominantly 16th-note rhythm, starting with the tonic (I) chord, C. After using common voicings for the iii (Em) and vi (Am) chords, the IV (F) chord is tackled with a six-string barre-chord voicing that should look familiar. On beats 2 and 4 of each measure, use a downstroke for the eighth note and a down-up combo for the 16th notes.

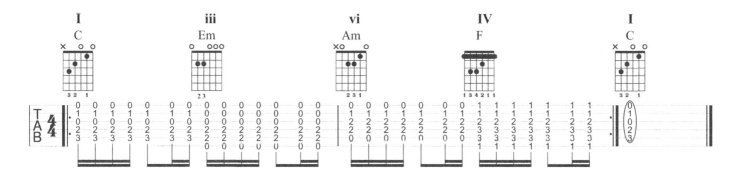

OPEN-CHORD ARPEGGIOS (1:15–1:00)

To arpeggiate our I–iii–vi–IV progression, played here in the key of G, we're going to alternate short, three-note ascending and descending patterns. The G (I) and Em (vi) chords feature a pattern that starts with their respective root notes and then jumps to string 3 for a three-note sweep of strings 3–1. Meanwhile, Bm (iii) and C (IV) use a similar pattern, only the notes on the top strings are played in reverse order, starting with string 1. These chord changes come at you fast, so be sure to start with a very slow tempo, increasing your speed incrementally.

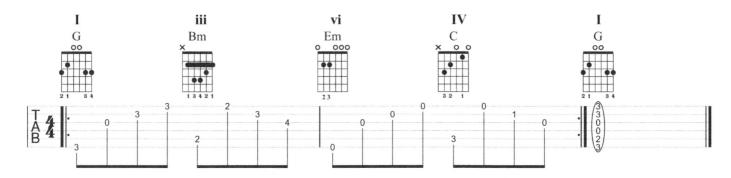

OPEN-CHORD FINGERPICKING (1:00–0:45)

The Travis-picking exercise featured here is an extension of yesterday's example. Whereas a pinch was used on only the first beat of each chord change in the previous exercise, this example features pinches on every beat (twice per chord). In spite of the additional pinches, the alternating-thumb pattern remains consistent throughout.

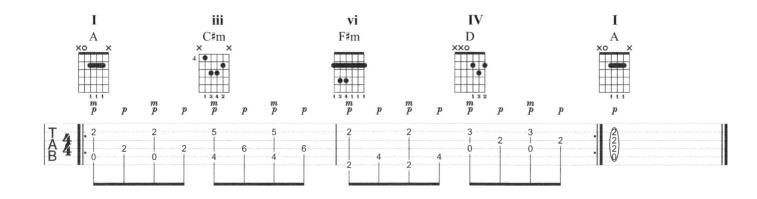

BARRE CHORDS (0:45–0:30)

In this exercise, the I–iii–vi–IV progression is tackled with a trio of six-string major and minor barre chords. The only exception is Dm, which is voiced on string 5. This Dm shape is almost identical to the Cm7 voicing we learned yesterday, only the pinky is added to string 3 to make it a minor triad instead of a minor seventh chord.

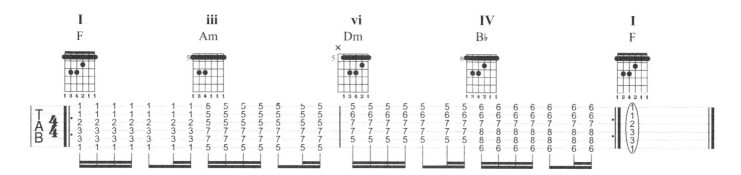

EXTENDED CHORDS (0:30–0:15)

This exercise features one new voicing that we haven't yet encountered: a major seventh voiced on string 6 (played here as Bbmaj7). This is a very common voicing for major seventh, so it's important to get to know it well. The other three chords—Dm7, Gm7, and Ebmaj7—are handled with voicings that we've used previously.

Rhythmically, the exercise is a bit different from the previous extended-chord examples in that eighth notes are featured on beat 2 of each measure. Since this is a jazzy example, be sure to swing those eighth notes; that is, play the first one a tab bit longer than the second (this is indicated by the notes in parentheses above the Bbmaj7 chord frame).

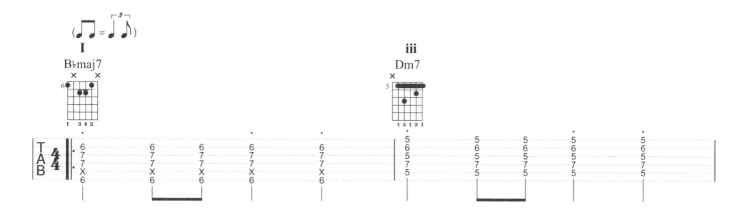

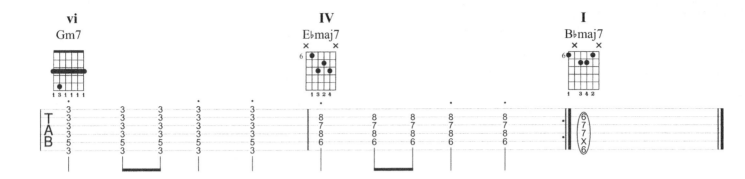

6/8 METER (0:15–0:00)

We're going to incorporate a couple of new techniques into this example. First up is the first-string pull-off in measure 1, and the second one is the pared-down F#m barre chord in measure 2.

Making the D-to-F#m change is a challenge due to having to fret the D note (fret 3, string 2) on the measure's final beat. To alleviate this problem (if, in fact, it is a problem) is to simply play the string open. Fortunately, this note, B, also belongs to the exercise's key, D major. The result is a slightly different "color," but, because it passes so quickly, it's negligible.

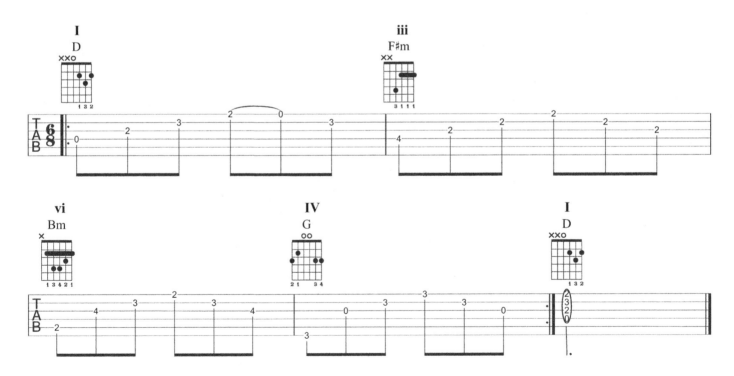

28

DAY 5: vi–V–IV–I PROGRESSION

If you're thinking, "*Hmm*, I thought we were working on major progressions, but this one starts on a minor chord," you're probably not alone. Sometimes progressions (and songs) are not firmly rooted in a major or minor key. In fact, it's not uncommon for a song's verse to be written in a minor key but switch to the relative major for the chorus, or vice versa.

Here, the vi–V–IV–I progression starts with the relative minor (vi chord) but ends with the tonic (I chord). As long as the progression/song ultimately resolves to the I chord, and the song's melody clearly resolves to the I chord's tonic, then the progression is probably major. If, however, the progression circles back to the vi chord for resolution (and the melody ends on the tonic of the vi chord), then it's likely a minor progression. In short: major progressions can start on minor chords, and vice versa.

Although you won't hear the vi–V–IV–I progression as the foundation for entire verses or choruses as often as other sets of changes (the list below contains a few, however), it is great for resolving one section of a song while simultaneously creating anticipation for another (e.g., the chorus).

EXAMPLES IN POPULAR SONGS:
"All on Me" by Devin Dawson (Key of F)
"Laura Palmer" by Bastille (Key of Ab)
"Unsteady" by X Ambassadors (Key of D)

OPEN-CHORD STRUMMING (1:30–1:15)

One reason the vi–V–IV–I progression is so effective at anticipating resolution to the tonic (I) chord are the consecutive whole steps that occur between the vi, V and IV chords. In the example below, this whole-step movement is emphasized by eighth-note stabs of the root notes, which are followed by full strums of the voicings. Notice the momentum that is created as the progression moves from vi to V to IV and, finally, to I.

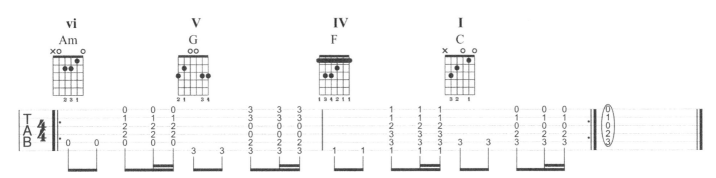

29

OPEN-CHORD ARPEGGIOS (1:15–1:00)

This next example gives us our first taste of syncopation. Instead of a steady stream of eighth notes, a tie appears on the "and" of beat 2 in each measure, which holds the note into beat 3, thereby creating some syncopation (i.e., the next note is played on a weak beat–the "and" of beat 3). The first half of each chord's arpeggio pattern consists of a series of string skips, followed in the second half by three notes that alternate on adjacent strings.

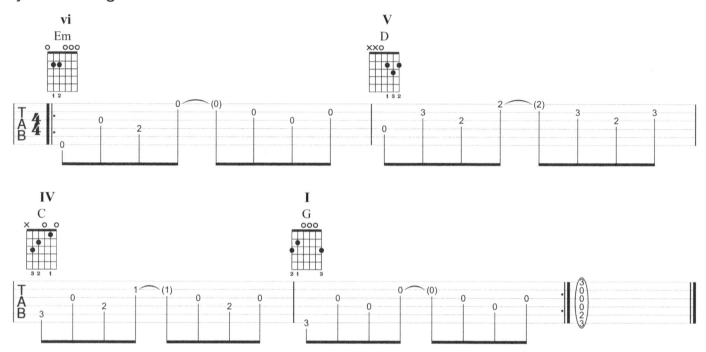

OPEN-CHORD FINGERPICKING (1:00–0:45)

This figure is an extension of yesterday's fingerpicking exercise. Like that example, this figure features pinches on beats 1 and 3 (each chord change), but now 16th notes are used on beats 2 and 4 to give the music a little more momentum. In spite of the rhythmic change, the thumb pattern remains consistent; that is, like the other Travis-picking exercises, the thumb alternates strings in a steady eighth-note rhythm.

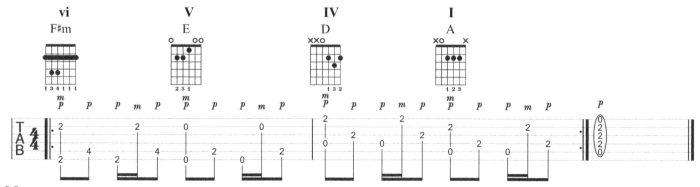

BARRE CHORDS (0:45–0:30)

Syncopation is also featured prominently is this next exercise. Instead of eighth-note syncopation like earlier, this figure is mostly strummed in a 16th-note rhythm, with a tie appearing at the end of beat 2, connecting the last 16th of that beat and the first one of beat 3. The rhythm is challenging at first, so be sure to listen to the audio demo to hear how it should sound.

Also of note is the F major barre chord. This is the major version of the fifth-string minor barre-chord shape we've encountered in previous exercises. This one is a little trickier than the minor version, however, because you must flatten out your ring finger to barre strings 2–4. If this voicing is new to you, and it gives you trouble, you can just play it as a power chord (strings 5–3) until your able to include the note on string 2.

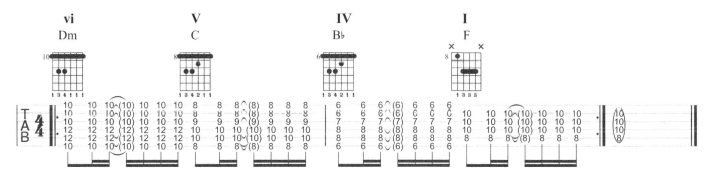

EXTENDED CHORDS (0:30–0:15)

After several jazz-style extended-chord exercises, we're going to change things up a bit. In this next example, major, minor, and dominant seventh chords are performed in a funky 16th-note "scratch" rhythm. The chords start in 10th position (Gm7) and work their way down the neck in whole-step increments until the I chord (Bbmaj7) arrives, at which point the exercise jumps to string 6 for resolution.

For the chord scratches, simply relieve some of your fret-hand pressure—without fully removing your hand from the strings. The result should be scratchy, percussive, toneless chords.

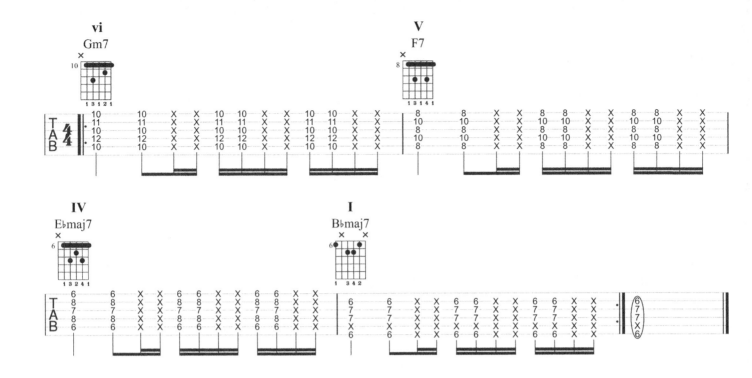

6/8 METER (0:15–0:00)

Today's 6/8 exercise combines two techniques: arpeggios and strumming. The arpeggios are performed in the first half of each measure and are followed by (slightly) syncopated chord strumming in the second half. For each chord, pluck the first note with a downstroke and arpeggiate through the subsequent two notes with a single upstroke. This will put your hand in an advantageous position to perform the first chord strum with a downstroke.

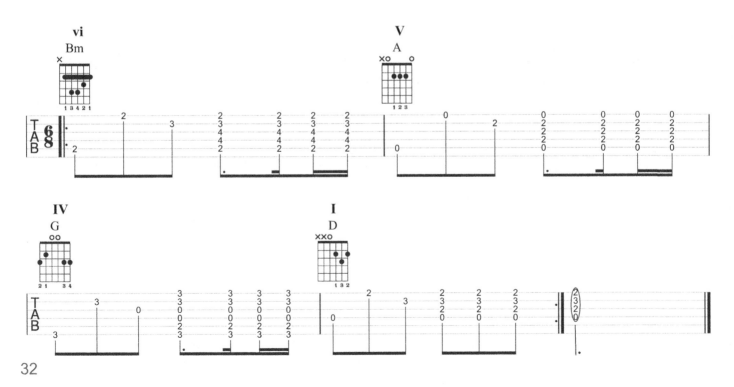

32

Known as the "classic rock" progression due to its popularity among hard rock groups in the '70s and '80s, I–bVII–IV–I remains a go-to progression for artists of all music genres to this day, including pop diva Lady Gaga, who scored a #1 smash with the progression (in the key of F#) on her track "Born This Way."

The I–bVII–IV–I progression is the first non-diatonic progression that we'll explore. This set of changes contains just one non-diatonic chord (bVII), but it doesn't really sound "outside," which is probably why so many artists gravitate to it. If you recall from the book's intro, the seventh chord of the harmonized major scale is a diminished triad (viidim), a chord not often heard in popular music.

In the I–bVII–IV–I progression, a major triad played a whole step (two frets) below the tonic (I) chord is used in lieu of the diatonic diminished chord (which is only a half step from the tonic). For example, in the key of C, instead of C–Bdim–F–C, we'd play C–Bb–F–C, a set of changes with a much more radio-friendly sound.

EXAMPLES IN POPULAR SONGS:
"I Can't Explain" by The Who (Key of E)
"Nothin' But a Good Time" by Poison (Key of Ab)
"Sweet Child O' Mine" by Guns N' Roses (Key of Db)
"Sweet Home Alabama" by Lynyrd Skynyrd (Key of D)

OPEN-CHORD STRUMMING (1:30–1:15)

Now we're going to put to work the C–Bb–F–C progression that we just discussed. In the following example, the chord changes are played in a rhythm that is similar to the one used in the Barre Chords section from yesterday. The main differences are the syncopated 16th notes on beat 1 of each measure, as well as the rests that appear on beat 2, which result in even more syncopation. For these rests, gently place your pick-hand palm onto the strings after the 16th-note (up)strum to stop the strings from ringing.

We also encounter a new chord voicing, Bbsus2, in this exercise. A sus2 (suspended 2nd) chord is a voicing that is comprised of the root, 2nd, and 5th of its relative scale. Because it omits the 3rd, the chord is neither major nor minor, but in the case of our example below, Bbsus2 is substituted for a major triad (Bb).

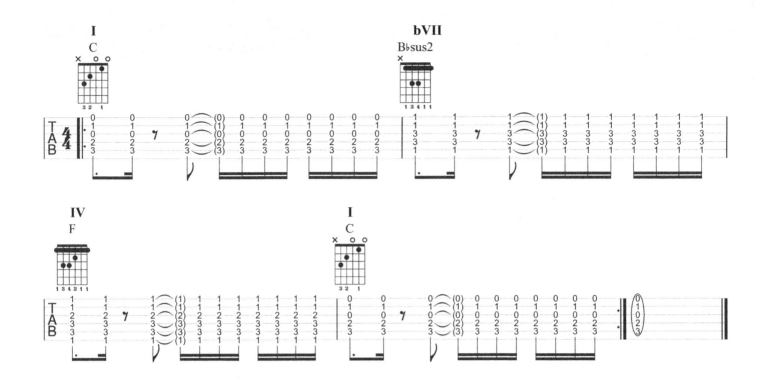

OPEN-CHORD ARPEGGIOS (1:15–1:00)

This arpeggio exercise does a fantastic job of showcasing the classic-rock vibe of the I–bVII–IV–I progression because it sounds like it could be taken from any number of songs from that era. All three chords—G, F, and C—are treated to the same arpeggio pattern, although the F chord is voiced on a higher string set. Start each chord with a downstroke, following it with a single upstroke for the two notes that immediately follow. Next, use a downstroke for the hammer-on and an upstroke for the eighth note that follows on the upbeat. Repeat this picking pattern for each chord.

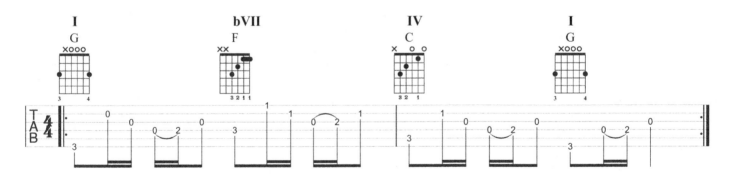

OPEN-CHORD FINGERPICKING (1:00–0:45)

Travis picking is the focus of today's fingerpicking exercise, as well. This time, however, we're going to move the pinches from beats 1 and 3 to beats 2 and 4. This seemingly small change creates a much different feel, so don't get discouraged if you struggle with it at first. The fingerings are provided above the tab staff, but feel free to experiment, using whatever feels most natural to you.

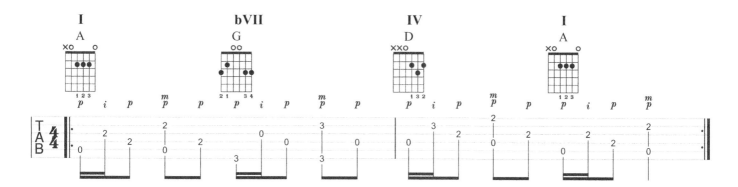

BARRE CHORDS (0:45–0:30) 🔊

This exercise features several barre-chord types. The first two chords, F and Eb, are based on an open C chord. The index finger is used in this voicing in place of the guitar's nut. Similarly, the Bb chord is based on an open G chord, with the index finger replacing the nut here, as well. The final F chord should look familiar because it's the six-string version we've used several time previously. By using this voicing, the root movement of the chord progression continues downward rather than having to jump back up the neck for resolution.

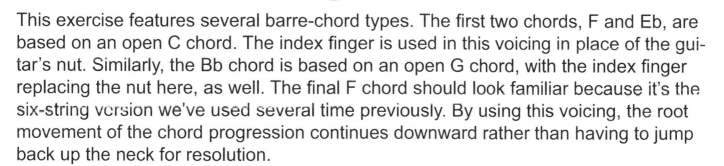

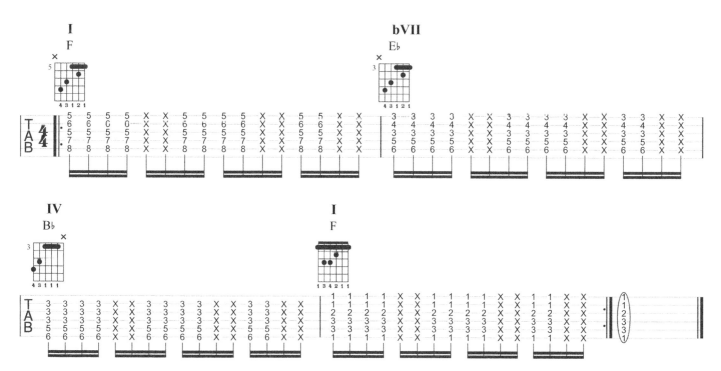

EXTENDED CHORDS (0:30–0:15)

This chord riff has a distinct modern pop sound. Here, major seventh and major ninth voicings are used to perform the I–bVII–IV–I progression. Rhythmically, the example alternates between rapid 16th-note arpeggiations and quarter-note rests, which give listeners time to digest each change in harmony. Like the previous exercise, an alternate I (Bb) chord voicing is used to cap the progression, allowing the root movement to continue its descent.

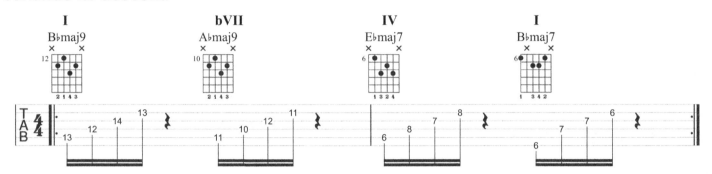

6/8 METER (0:15–0:00)

Chord ornamentation is the focal point of today's 6/8 exercise. While all the voicings are common open chords, each one is embellished with a hammer-on and open strings. For the D (I) chord, the embellishments occur on string 1, where a short little melody is created. In measures 2–3, the Cadd9 (bVII) and G (IV) chords feature hammer-ons on strings 4 and 5, respectively. Be sure to listen to the audio to hear a demonstration of the exercise.

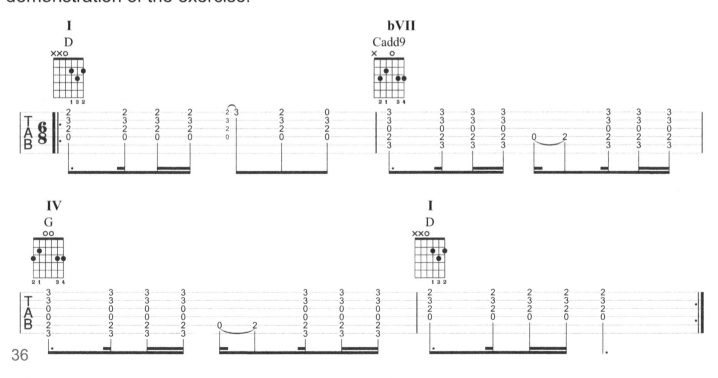

Today, we're going to tackle our second non-diatonic progression, I–V–IV–iv. The popularity of this progression exploded in the '60s, when the Beatles began incorporating the changes—and variations of them—into their music. The first three chords—I, V, and IV—are diatonic to the major scale, but the final chord, iv, is not. This major IV to minor iv change (the latter of which is borrowed from the harmonized relative minor scale) gives the progression a unique, melancholic sound, which is great for resolving one section of a song and signaling the arrival of another.

Although we'll be playing I–V–IV–iv here, you'll often come across variations of this progression that start with chords other than I–V or simply feature a different order of the chords (such as some of the songs listed below), but what does remain consistent is the IV to iv change because those chords, in that order, gives the progression its character.

EXAMPLES IN POPULAR SONGS:
"Blackbird" by the Beatles (Key of F)
"Don't Look Back in Anger" by Oasis (Key of C)
"In My Life" by The Beatles (Key of A)
"Nobody Home" by Pink Floyd (Key of C)
"Speechless" by Dan + Shay (key of C#)
"Wake Me When September Ends" by Green Day (Key of G)

OPEN-CHORD STRUMMING (1:30–1:15)

Today, we're going to deviate from traditional strumming a bit in order to work on a technique that has become immensely popular in pop and rock music: percussive fingerstyle. *Percussive fingerstyle* involves plucking the notes of the chords with the pick-hand fingers and then percussively smacking the strings with the same hand (on beats 2 and 4). The resultant sound is similar to the muted chords we've worked on previously, only here we're using the fingers/hand instead of the pick. To best way to execute these percussive strokes is to release fret-hand pressure from the chord while simultaneously allowing your pick hand to come down onto the strings (over the soundhole/ pickups) with moderate force.

In the example below, use all five of your fingers to pluck the open C chord, then bring your hand down onto the strings on the next beat (beat 2). Immediately after striking the deadened strings, pluck the chord again (on the "and" of beat 2), holding the chord through beat 3. Finally, strike the strings once again, this time on beat 4. Use this pattern for the remaining three chords (G5, F, and Fm).

These percussive "hits" mimic the sound of a snare drum, allowing you to really lock into the groove. You can also try streamlining the chords a bit and pluck only three or four notes of the chord instead of five (for some, incorporating the pinky can be challenging).

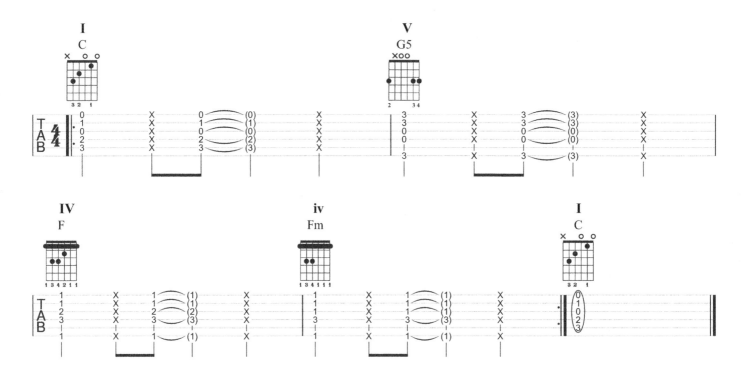

OPEN-CHORD ARPEGGIOS (1:15–1:00)

Today's arpeggio pattern incorporates a couple of techniques that we've covered in previous lessons: syncopation and hammer-ons. The syncopation here is created by a tie that connects the "and" of beat 2 to the downbeat of beat 3, thereby requiring a string pluck on the weak beat ("and" of beat 3). This is followed by a hammer-on from an open string to a fretted pitch of the chord voicing, a move that is mimicked in each measure.

The trickiest part of this progression is moving from the major IV to the minor iv because it requires shifting from an open chord (C) to a five-string barre chord (Cm). Fortunately, the note at the end of measure 3, G, is an open string, so use this to your advantage when making the change; in other words, you have half a beat (the duration of one eighth note) to move from C to Cm.

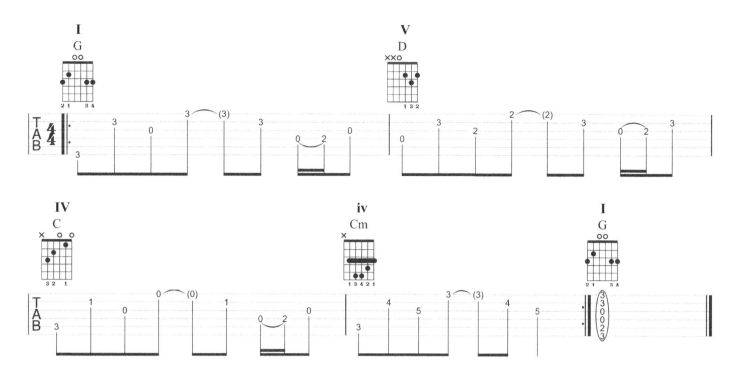

OPEN-CHORD FINGERPICKING (1:00–0:45)

Once again, Travis picking is the focal point of our fingerpicking exercise. This time, however, the pitches occur on weak beats ("and" of beats 1 and 3) throughout. This may feel a bit awkward at first, but once you get comfortable with the pick-hand fingerings, it will start to feel more natural. Like all of our Travis-picking patterns, the alternating thumb is consistent throughout, so start with that finger, plucking the bass strings in a steady eighth-note rhythm while incorporating the other fingers incrementally.

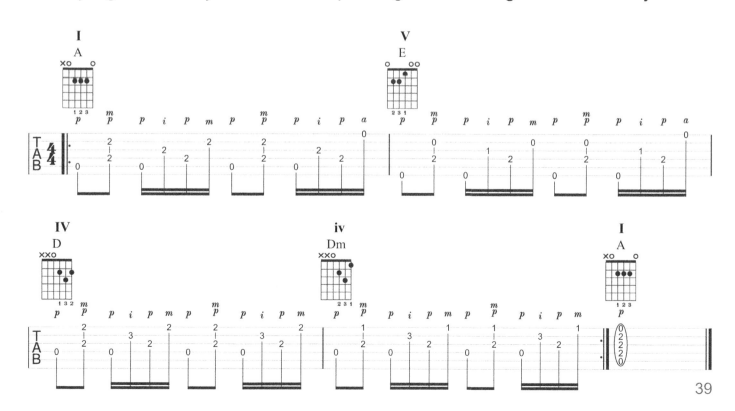

BARRE CHORDS (0:45–0:30)

This exercise features both six- and five-string barre-chord shapes, which are stated at the opening of each measure and then followed by 16th-note drones of the root notes. Notice that, outside of the I (F) chord, the voicings are strummed in an anticipatory fashion, coming in one 16th note prior to the downbeat (beat 1). Strum the F chord with a downstroke, then use alternate (down-up-down-up) picking for the root-note drones, including the syncopated chord stabs at the end of the measures, which should be struck with an upstroke.

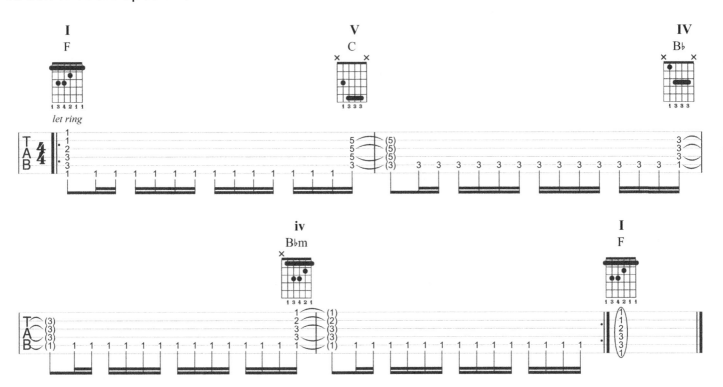

EXTENDED CHORDS (0:30–0:15)

This jazzy extended-chord exercise features voicings that we've encountered previous-ly, as well as a couple of new ones, F13 and F9. The F9 voicing is the most common way to play a dominant ninth chord on guitar. Meanwhile, the F13 chord, while a popu-lar voicing in and of itself, is used here to provide some melodic movement during the V-chord harmony. To execute this change, start by getting comfortable with the F9 voic-ing, using your ring finger to barre strings 1–3. Once you have that chord under your belt, simply reach up to fret 10 with your pinky to turn it into F13. Removing your pinky from string 1 is all that is needed to change from F13 to F9.

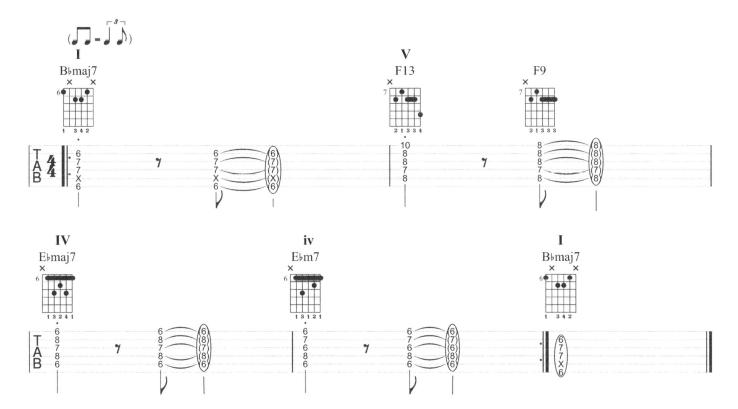

6/8 METER (0:15–0:00)

This example is a pretty straightforward arpeggiation of the I–V–IV–iv progression, except for the V (A) chord change, which features melodic movement within the voicing not unlike what we experienced in our previous exercise (F13 to F9). For the G to Gm change, use a three-string barre for the G chord so you can simply lift your middle finger from string 3 to turn it into Gm.

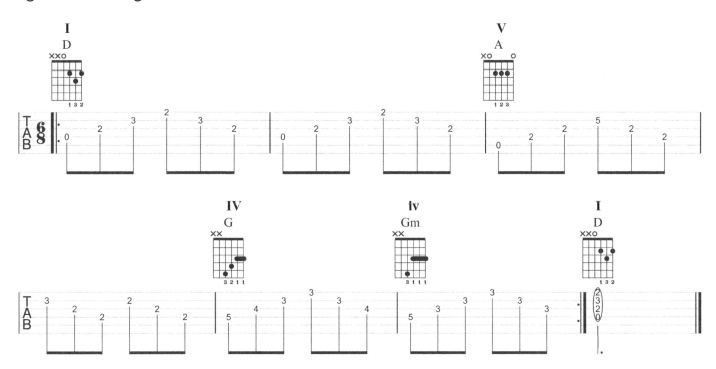

DAY 8: i–iv PROGRESSION

The i–iv progression is the minor-key version of the I–IV progression that we learned on Day 1. The distance between the roots of the two chords (a perfect 4th) is exactly the same, but now both voicings are minor (rather than major).

The minor i–iv is found in all styles of music, from pop and rock to jazz and reggae, either as a "standalone" progression or as part of a broader set of changes. For example, the chorus to Bob Marley's classic "I Shot the Sheriff" is a straight i–iv in the key of G minor: Gm–Cm. Alternately, Justin Bieber's pop hit "Boyfriend" is based on a four-chord progression that commences with the i–iv change: Bbm–Ebm–Ab–Db (i–iv–VII–III in Bb minor). And we can't discuss the minor i–iv without specifically mentioning the blues because nearly every minor-key blues tune features the i–iv progression prominently.

EXAMPLES IN POPULAR SONGS:
"Bring Me to Life" by Evanescence (Key of E Minor)
"Since I've Been Loving You" by Led Zeppelin (Key of C Minor)
"The Thrill Is Gone" by B.B. King (Key of B Minor)
"Tin Pan Alley" by Stevie Ray Vaughan (Key of B Minor)

OPEN-CHORD STRUMMING (1:30–1:15)

Percussive strums on the backbeat (beats 2 and 4) are the distinguishing feature of this next exercise. This technique is similar to the percussive fingerstyle approach that we worked on yesterday, but instead of creating the faux snare sound by smacking the strings over the pickups/soundhole with our pick hand, here we're going to strum through the strings while simultaneously muting them with the blade of our pick hand— all in one motion. Harmonically, the changes are pretty straightforward: an open Am chord to an open Dm chord.

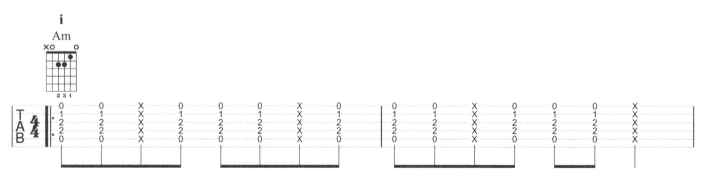

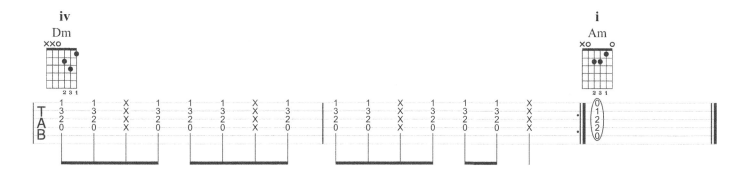

OPEN-CHORD ARPEGGIOS (1:15–1:00)

The biggest challenge of this next exercise is executing the rhythm in time. Although the rhythm is straight 16th notes, the three-note groupings on the treble strings create a three-against-four "polyrhythm."

Pluck the first (root) note of each chord with a downstroke. Then arpeggiate the subsequent three notes with three straight upstrokes (which are really just one broad upstroke through the top three strings). Use this technique for each of the three-note groupings throughout.

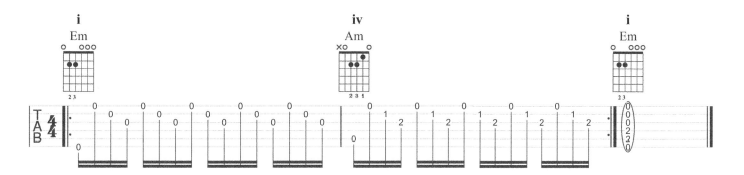

OPEN-CHORD FINGERPICKING (1:00–0:45)

The fingerpicking pattern we'll be using in the exercise below is influenced by classical guitar. Following each pinch (on beats 1 and 3), an index-middle-index picking pattern is utilized on strings 3 and 2. The pattern is consistent throughout, with the only adjustment coming from the thumb, which has to move from string 6 to string 5 for the iv (Bm7) chord. For the sake of efficiency, keep your index-finger barre in place when moving from F#m to Bm7. Although string 6 is note part of the Bm7 voicing (you won't pluck it), keeping the barre in place prevents you from having to adjust your entire fret hand when moving back and forth between the two chords.

43

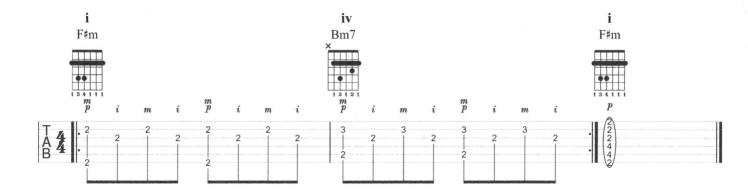

BARRE CHORDS (0:45–0:30)

This funky, Doobie Brothers-esque exercise features a single minor seventh voicing that is used for both the i and the iv chord. Likewise, the rhythm used in measure 1 is also repeated in measure 2, so once you get the i (Dm7) chord change under your belt, simply move the voicing up to fret 10 and play the same rhythm. The tricky part of the exercise is the syncopation that is created by the chord scratches. Listen to the audio demonstration to help you get the feel.

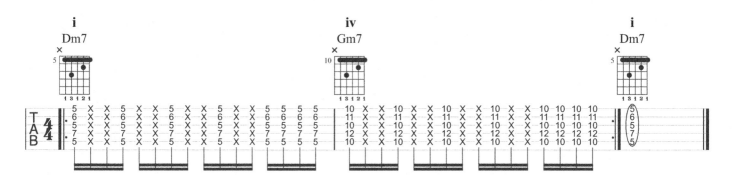

EXTENDED CHORDS (0:30–0:15)

We're going to learn a couple of new chord voicings in this section, one for minor seventh chords and one for minor ninths. The i–iv progression is played here in the key of G minor, with the minor seventh voicing handling the i-chord change, and the minor ninth voicing handling the iv chord. Both voicings are a little tricky for those unfamiliar, so don't get discouraged if you struggle with them at first. Also: be sure to swing those eighth notes!

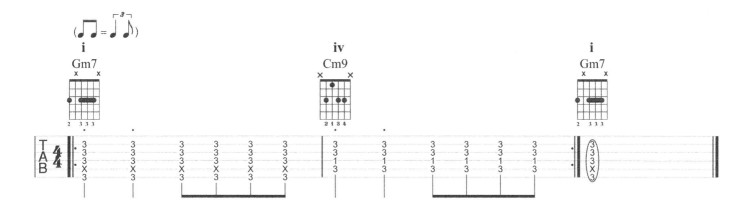

6/8 METER (0:15–0:00)

We're going to stick with the "new chord voicings" theme in this section, as well. Here, we're going to learn one that's relatively uncommon (Bm7) and one that is quite popular (Em7). When moving from Bm7 to Em7, keep your index and pinky fingers in place, adjusting only your middle (moving it from string 3 to string 4) and ring (lifting it from string 1) fingers.

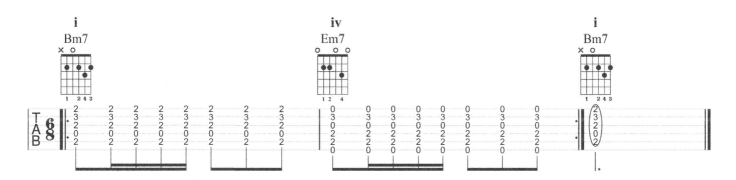

This progression, i–v–iv–i, is the minor version of the I–V–IV progression that we learned on Day 2. All of the root movement is the same, but now the chords are minor instead of major. Although you'll hear these changes in all kinds of minor-key blues tunes, the i–v–iv–I progression doesn't get nearly the airtime of its major counterpart. Nevertheless, these minor changes are important to get acclimated to in order to further develop your ear because, for most people, hearing major changes comes pretty naturally, whereas minor progression feel a bit more foreign.

EXAMPLES IN POPULAR SONGS:

"Ain't No Sunshine" by Bill Withers (Key of A Minor)
"Cake by the Ocean" by DNCE (Key of E Minor)
Most Minor-Key Blues Turnarounds (last four bars of the 12-bar song form)

OPEN-CHORD STRUMMING (1:30–1:15)

This next exercise involves some syncopated chord strumming, as well as a heavy dose of scratch chords. We're going to use two approaches to the chord scratches. For the ones that appear on beat 2, use the blade of your pick hand to mute the strum; for the quick 16th-note mutes on beat 4, lightly lay your fret-hand fingers across the strings, using them to achieve the percussive sound.

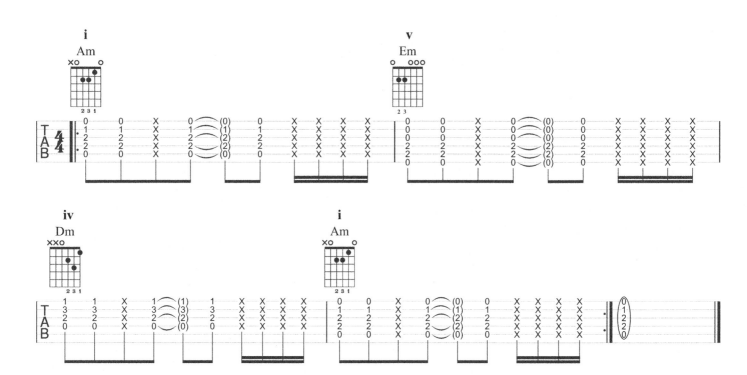

OPEN-CHORD ARPEGGIOS (1:15–1:00)

The distinguishing features of this figure include a repetitive arpeggio pattern and a pair of pull-offs that give the Bm (v) and Am (iv) chords a suspended (sus2) sound. You can choose to voice the Am chord one of two ways: 1) by using the fingering suggested in the chord frame above the tab staff, or 2) by sliding the Bm voicing down two frets and using your ring (string 4), pinky (string 3), and middle (string 2) fingers, letting your index finger hover above the nut.

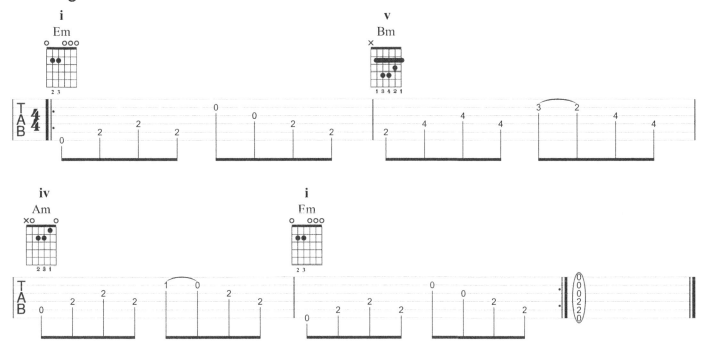

OPEN-CHORD FINGERPICKING (1:00–0:45)

This fingerpicking exercise alternates thumb-middle pinches and index finger plucks of the third string. This example has a classical-guitar feel, partly due to the minor tonality, but the alternating thumb pattern gives it a country vibe, as well, albeit a slight one. As with all of our fingerpicking exercises, feel free to experiment with fingerings. The ones included in the tab are merely suggestions.

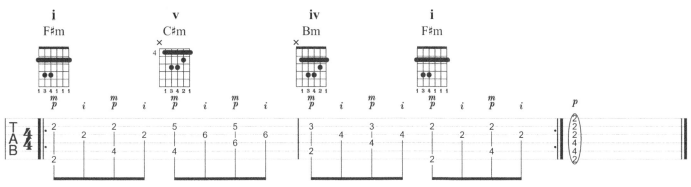

BARRE CHORDS (0:45–0:30)

While barre chords are the focus, this next exercise has a lot more going on. The voicings used here are six- and five-string minor sevenths that we've encountered previously, but what gives this example is unique sound is the use of space (i.e., rests), a part of the musical equation that is too often overlooked. Also of note is the short little guitar lick used to punctuate the progression. Fortunately, this lick is played in-position, so you don't have to move your fret hand when moving between the Dm7 chord and the single notes.

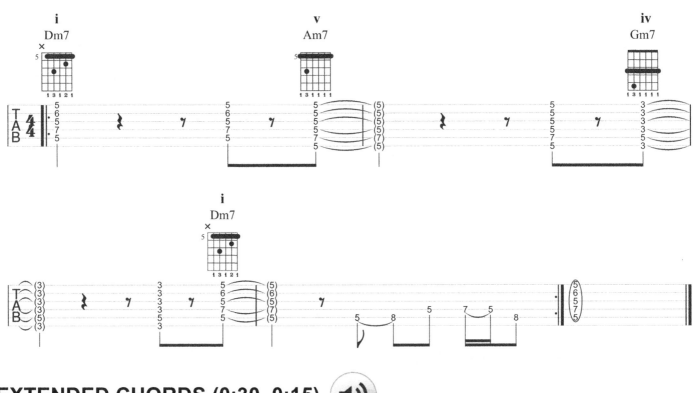

EXTENDED CHORDS (0:30–0:15)

In this section, we're going to perform the i–v–iv–i progression with a couple of new voicings, which will enable us to punctuate each chord change with its own short melodic line. The first chord, Gm9, is voiced on the top four strings with an index-finger barre, with the ring finger reaching up to fret 5 of string 1 to grab the 9th (A). The next two chords, Dm7 and Cm7, are a little trickier. The voicings are similar to the standard five-string minor seventh barre chord, except here the high b7th is included in each chord (on string 1).

The rhythms of the single-note lines are a bit challenging, as well. These quarter-note triplets involve playing three notes in the space of two beats, creating a three-against-two polyrhythm. If quarter-note triplets are new to you, be sure to listen to the audio demonstration.

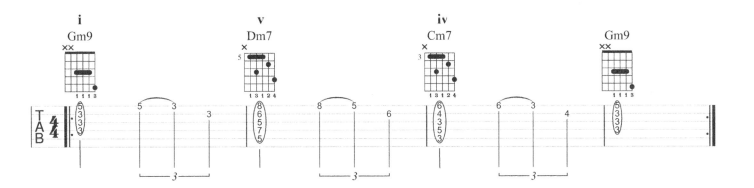

6/8 METER (0:15–0:00)

The strumming in this 6/8 example is pretty straightforward, as are the chords, despite the scary names of a couple of them. The Bm(add11) chord is simply a standard Bm chord with the open high E string (the 11th) included. Similarly, the F#m11 chord is just a variation of a standard F#m chord, with open strings substituted for an index-finger barre at fret 2.

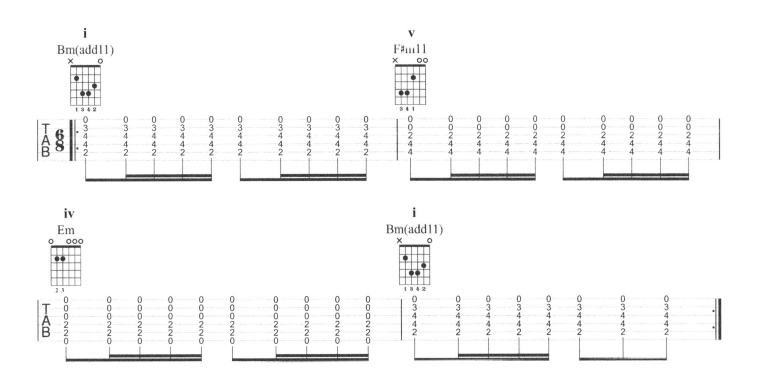

DAY 10: i–VII–VI–VII PROGRESSION

After two days of playing nothing but minor chords, in this lesson, we're going to work on a minor progression that incorporates two major chords, i–VII–VI–VII. What you may have noticed about this set of changes is that, after moving to the VI chord, the progression cycles back to the VII chord again. Up to this point, we haven't encountered a progression that repeats one or more of its chords, but it's something you should explore when building your own set of changes. Recycling changes in multichord progressions is common practice in all styles of music.

EXAMPLES IN POPULAR SONGS:
"All Along the Watchtower" by Bob Dylan (Key of C# Minor)
"In the Air Tonight" by Phil Collins (Key of D Minor)
"Rolling in the Deep" by Adele (Key of C Minor)
"Somebody That I Used to Know" by Gotye (Key of D Minor)
"Starboy" by The Weeknd (Key of A Minor)

OPEN-CHORD STRUMMING (1:30–1:15)

Syncopated and percussive chord strumming is the focal point of this i–VII–VI–VII progression played in the key of A minor. Feel free to experiment with the fingering for the G chord. A ring-pinky combo is suggested here, but a middle-ring or middle-pinky combo might feel more natural to you.

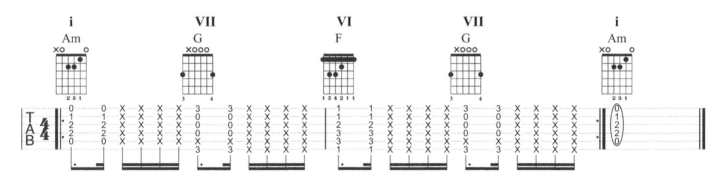

OPEN-CHORD ARPEGGIOS (1:15–1:00)

The i–VII–VI–VII progression is performed here with a trio of common open chords—Em (i), D (VII), and C (VI)—and a "jagged" arpeggio pattern that is mimicked in each measure. Notice in measure 1 that the fourth-string E (root) note is used instead of the open low E string. This is strategic, as it allows the roots of the chords to uniformly descend/ascend in whole steps (E–D–C–D) on strings 4 and 5.

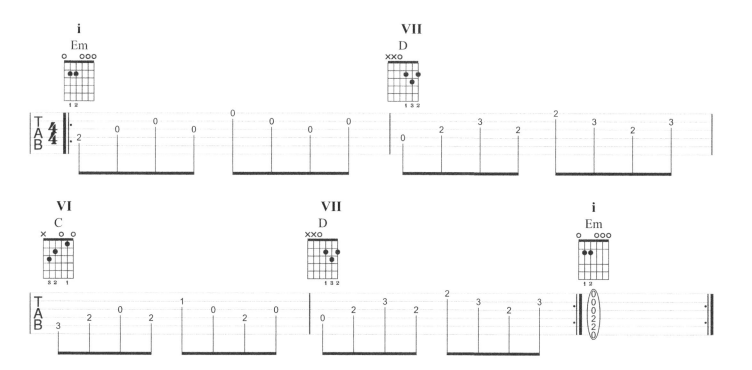

OPEN-CHORD FINGERPICKING (1:00–0:45)

This fingerpicking pattern, which alternates middle-index plucks of the treble strings with thumb plucks of the bass strings, is reminiscent of the piano riffs heard in songs like the Beatles' "Let it Be" and Coldplay's "The Scientist, among many others.

When moving from F#m to E, an alternate fingering approach to the one suggested in the chord diagrams is to slide your ring and pinky fingers from fret 4 to fret 2 and add your middle finger to fret 1 of string 3, thereby voicing the E chord with your ring, pinky, and middle fingers (low to high). Meanwhile, your index finger would simply hover above the guitar's nut.

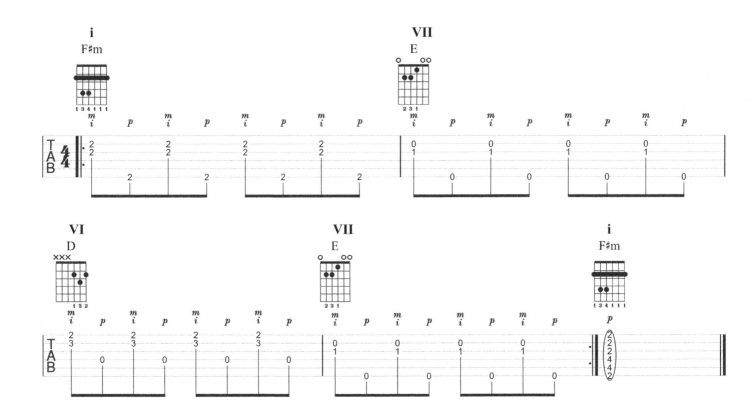

BARRE CHORDS (0:45–0:30)

Like our Barre Chords exercise from Day 8, this next example also has a bit of a Doobie Brothers vibe to it, thanks to the chordal hammer-ons.

The major barre-chord shape used for the VII and VI chords might look new to you, but it's actually a slightly smaller versions of one that we used back on Day 6 (for the Bb chord). For these two changes, C and Bb, barre strings 2–5 with your index finger while using your ring finger to execute the fifth-string hammer-on.

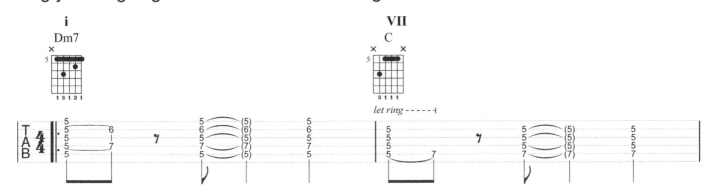

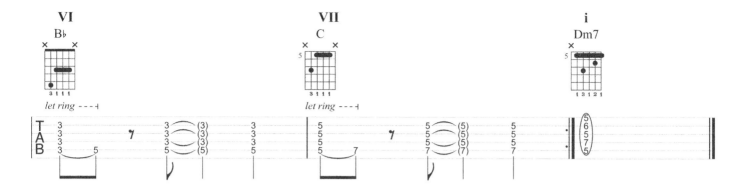

EXTENDED CHORDS (0:30–0:15)

This funky exercise performs the i–VII–VI–VII progression, played here in the key of G minor, with a trio of seventh-chord voicings that should be familiar to you by now. Notice that the VII (F7) and VI (Ebmaj7) chord changes occur on the "and" of beat 4 of the preceding measure. This slight bit of syncopation, which we've encountered in a few of our previous exercises, is a great way to inject some momentum into your chord changes because it creates a sense of anticipation that doesn't exist when playing each change directly on the downbeat.

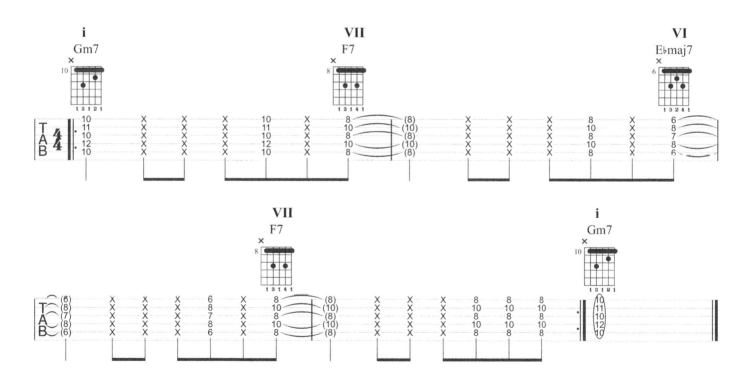

6/8 METER (0:15–0:00) 🔊

Six-string barre-chord shapes handle the harmony in this next example. Although no picking directions are included, you can experiment with fingerpicking this exercise, plucking the dyads on strings 2–3 with either an index-middle or a middle-ring finger combo. Speaking of dyads, be sure to give the dotted quarter notes a full three-beat ("4, 5, 6") count.

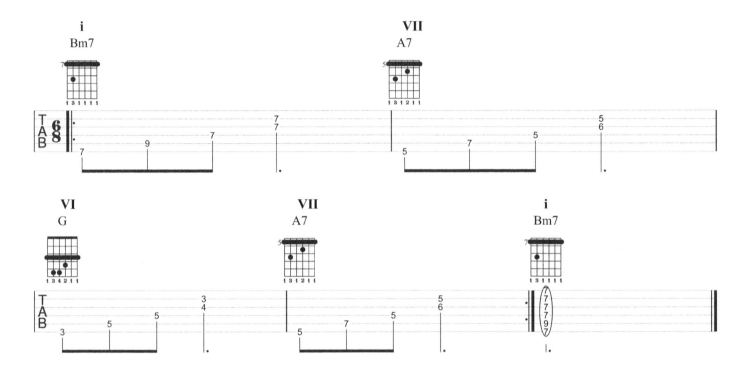

The i–VI–III–VII progression is used in just about every music genre—and perhaps to a greater degree than any other. Why? Well, because it sounds *so* good and just begs for a pop or rock hook to be written over the top of it!

Although we're going to analyze this set of chord changes as a minor progression, with the relative minor functioning as the i chord, we could also perceive the harmony as being major, so the i chord would receive its relative-minor label, vi, resulting in a vi–IV–I–V progression (notice that the III chord of the minor progression is now the relative major, or I chord). Sometimes determining whether a progression is major or minor is impossible in isolation; it really depends on the overall tonality of the music, particularly what notes the melody begins and ends on.

EXAMPLES IN POPULAR SONGS:
"Apologize" by OneRepublic (Key of C Minor)
"Behind These Hazel Eyes" by Kelly Clarkson (Key of F# Minor)
"Numb" by Linkin Park (Key of F# Minor)
"Save Tonight" by Eagle-Eye Cherry (Key of A Minor)
"Self Esteem" by The Offspring (Key of A Minor)
"The Scientist" by Coldplay (Key of D Minor)
"Zombie" by The Cranberries (Key of E Minor)

OPEN-CHORD STRUMMING (1:30–1:15)

This example is a variation on the strumming exercise from yesterday. The main differences in this example is the syncopation created by the ties and the absence of percussive strums. The syncopation is a bit tricky, so listen to the accompanying audio to hear how it should be performed.

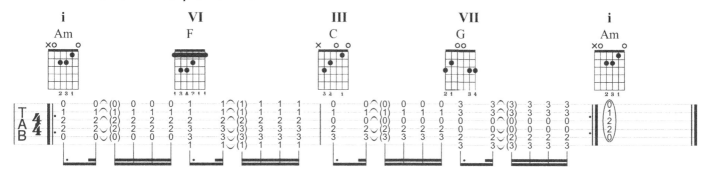

OPEN-CHORD ARPEGGIOS (1:15–1:00)

The arpeggio pattern used here is one we've explored previously, so it should feel familiar. However, the progression does have a unique sound due its voicings, each of which incorporates the open G string, which is allowed to drone throughout.

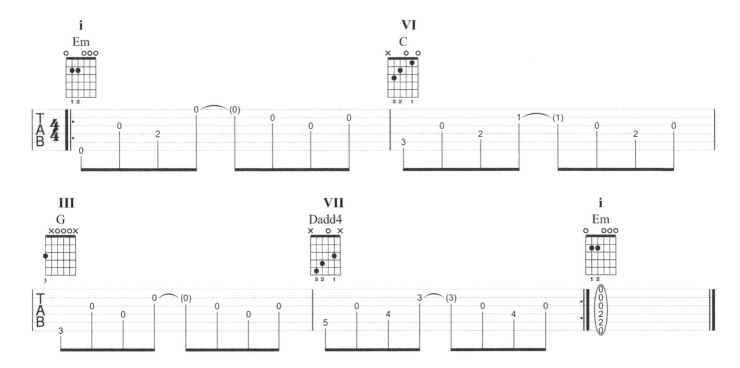

OPEN-CHORD FINGERPICKING (1:00–0:45)

This next example has a distinct pop sound and feel. In addition to the quick, 16th-note arpeggiations on beat 1 (heard often on pop radio right now), the progression also features the percussive fingerstyle technique that was introduced on Day 7.

Place a good bit of your focus on the arpeggiations, being sure not to rush the 16th notes. Each of the arpeggios is performed with a *p–i–m–a* (thumb–index–middle–ring) combination, which might feel a bit awkward at first, especially at this speed, so start slowly and increase your speed incrementally.

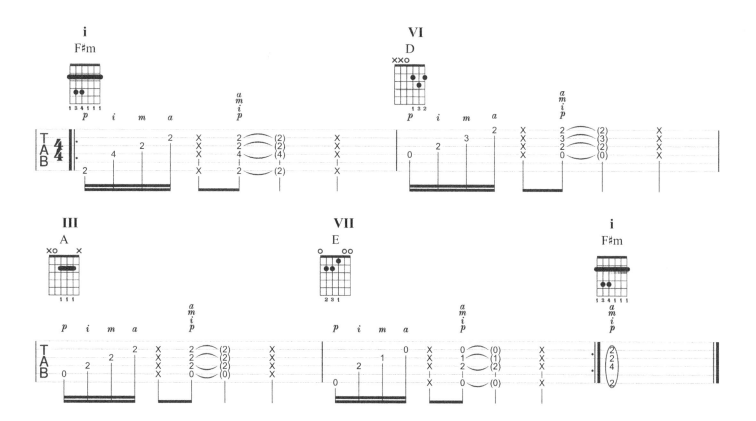

BARRE CHORDS (0:45–0:30)

Fifth- and sixth-string-root major and minor barre chords are alternated in this next exercise. Root-note palm mutes are used to drive home the chord changes at the top of each measure, and quick, 16th-note percussive strums offset the changes on beat 3. These scratch chords not only give the progression a syncopated feel, they provide your fret hand enough time to make the changes.

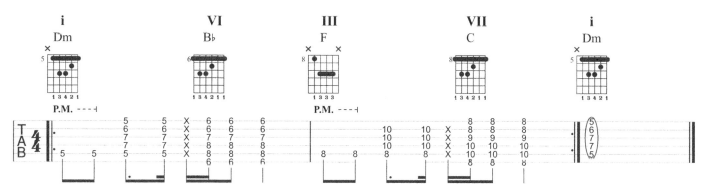

EXTENDED CHORDS (0:30–0:15)

The extended chords in this example are mainly voiced along string 5, the only exception being the Bbmaj7 chord, which is played on string 6. In addition to the challenges of playing the syncopated rhythm, some of these voicings can be tricky to play back to back, so take this one slow and steady. It might also be helpful to listen to the audio demonstration before tackling the exercise.

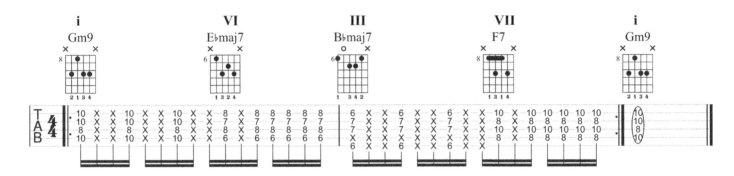

6/8 METER (0:15–0:00)

This 6/8 exercise is comprised of some common, and some not so common, voicings. Although performed in different keys, this example shares a feature with the music figure we explored earlier, in the Open-Chord Arpeggios section: a droning G string. Notice how, after three measures of the G string droning over the i–VI–III (Bm[addb6]–G–Dadd4) changes, the addition of the third-string A note in measure 4 (root of the Aadd4 chord) really stands out, lending some melodic heft to the proceedings.

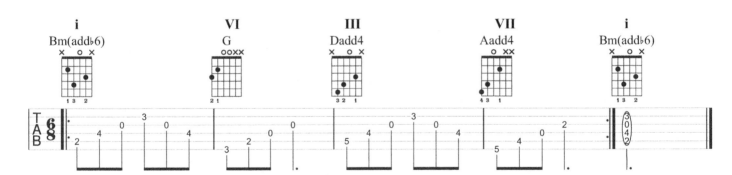

DAY 12: VI–III–VII–i PROGRESSION

Our next progression, VI–III–VII–i, should look familiar because it's the same progression that we learned yesterday, only we're starting on the VI chord rather than the tonic (i). Like major progressions, minor changes don't require us to start on the tonic chord; in fact, many popular minor progression start on chords other than the tonic. In yesterday's progression, we started on the i chord and ended on the VII; here, we're starting on the VI and *ending* on the i. This harmony, VI–III–VII–I, sounds great, so it's no surprise that it's a favorite among pop artists and songwriters (see list below).

EXAMPLES IN POPULAR SONGS:
"Bad Blood" by Taylor Swift (Key of E Minor)
"I Don't Wanna Live Forever" by ZAYN and Taylor Swift (Key of A Minor)
"I Really Like You" by Carly Rae Jepsen (Key of D Minor)

OPEN-CHORD STRUMMING (1:30–1:15)

We explored the technique of palm muting root notes in yesterday's Barre Chords section; today, we're going to expand on it a bit. Whereas palm mutes were incorporated only on beat 1 in yesterday's exercise, in the example below, we're going to play palm mutes on beats 1 and 3. Additionally, we're going to up the ante rhythmically by playing a "reverse gallop" on beat 3 of each measure instead of straight eighth notes. For these reverse gallops, use alternate picking, starting and ending the beat with a downstroke.

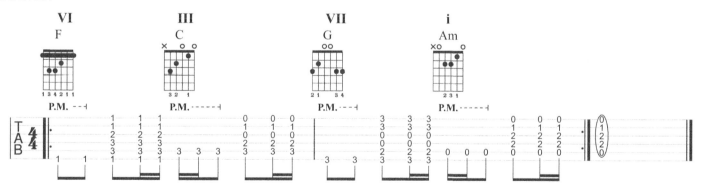

OPEN-CHORD ARPEGGIOS (1:15–1:00)

This next example has a country/folk vibe and involves arpeggiating open C, G, D, and Em voicings in a rhythm that combines eighth notes and 16ths. Notice in measure 1 that, despite the change in harmony (C to G), the hammer-on figure remains the same. Then, in measure 2, when the harmony changes to the VII (D) chord, the figure is "answered" by a similar pattern on strings 1–2 and then further embellished with a pull-off pattern over the i (Em) chord, which also signals a return to the progression's first chord, C. Don't be afraid to experiment with the fingerings here; for example, you might want to try using your ring finger to fret the root of the G chord (fret 3, string 6) since it's already being used to voice the root of the preceding C chord (fret 3, string 5). Efficiency is the goal of fret-hand fingerings.

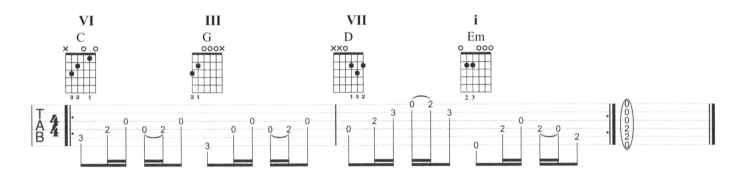

OPEN-CHORD FINGERPICKING (1:00–0:45)

The fingerpicking pattern used here is similar to ones we've used in the past, but what makes this one unique is the way the bass (root) notes are played with the thumb on both the downbeat of each change, as well as the eighth note preceding the next change. The result is a bit of syncopation in an otherwise (rhythmically) straightforward example.

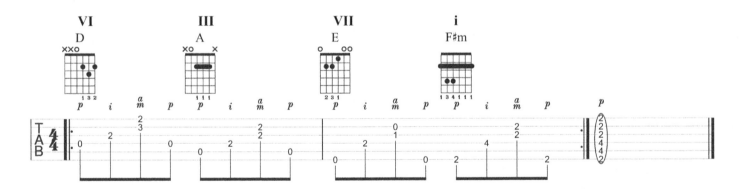

BARRE CHORDS (0:45–0:30)

This next example is one part John Frusciante (Red Hot Chili Peppers) and one part Jimi Hendrix. Rather than just stick to strumming barre chords for the VI–III–VII–i progression, played here in D minor, we're going to decorate the III and i chords with melodic embellishments.

In measure 1, after strumming (and holding) the F chord, slide your ring finger from fret 10 to fret 12 of the fifth string, using your index finger for the double stop. For the Dm chord, stay in position and use either your ring finger or your pinky for the hammer-on. If you choose the latter, you can essentially keep the chord fully voiced, using your ring finger for the 12th-fret slide.

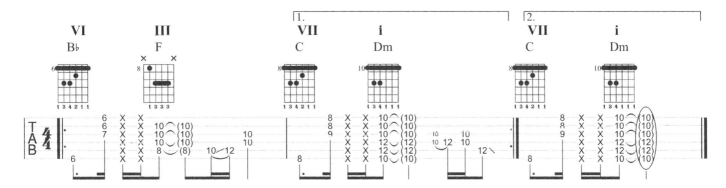

EXTENDED CHORDS (0:30–0:15)

Because it's such an amazing songwriting tool, we're going to incorporate syncopation once again, this time in a four-bar example that utilizes a plethora of extended chords, including a major ninth, dominant and minor sevenths, and a major sixth. Note that, after some straight-eighth-note strumming (and a rest) in measure 1, the sixth-string root of the Bb6 chord is plucked on the "and" of beat 4 in anticipation of the chord change. This same approach is used for the next two chords, F7 and Gm7, as well. As mentioned previously, this type of syncopation elevates the anticipation level of the chord changes and, in turn, the energy of the song.

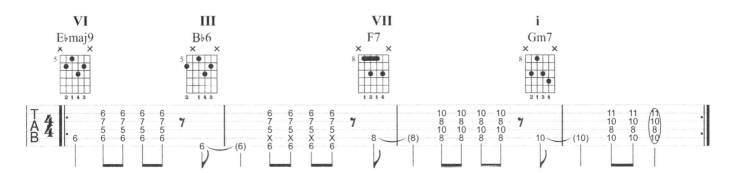

6/8 METER (0:15–0:00)

In addition to syncopation, another tool that can add some energy and excitement to an otherwise dull chord progression is *melody*. Embellishing chords with a few notes that fall outside the framework of the voicing is a technique that has stood the test of time, regardless of music genre.

In the exercise below, a descending G–F#–E melody is played on string 1 over the G (VI) and D (III) changes. Then, in measure 3, the A (VII) chord "answers" the initial melody with a short phrase of its own, played here on string 2. All of this resolves to a stock Bm (i) chord in measure 4. The strumming is pretty straightforward, so most of your focus can be placed on the embellishments.

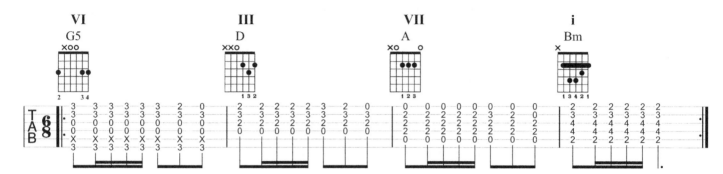

Up to this point, all of our minor progressions have been diatonic. Now, we're going to turn our attention to our first non-diatonic minor progression, i–III–IV–VI. In this progression, only one of the four chords, the IV, falls outside the key; the other three chords are part of the same family. For example, in the key of A minor, Dm is the diatonic iv chord. Here, however, the uppercase "IV" indicates that the chord is major; therefore, our i–III–IV–VI progression would be played as Am–C–**D**–F, rather than Am–C–Dm–F.

Unless your radio is tuned to a classic rock station, you probably won't hear the i–III–IV–VI progression in action very often, but it's worthy of study nonetheless because of the iconic status of some of the songs that have used it, or at least variations of it. Two prime examples include The Animals' "House of the Rising Sun" and Led Zeppelin's "Stairway to Heaven." Let's hear how this progression sounds in a half dozen of our own examples…

EXAMPLES IN POPULAR SONGS:
"House of the Rising Sun" by The Animals (Key of A Minor)
"Stairway to Heaven" by Led Zeppelin (Key of A Minor)

OPEN-CHORD STRUMMING (1:30–1:15)

Some of the voicings used in this next example are variations of chords we already know. For example, C/G is simply an open C chord with the 5th (G) played in the bass

(this type of voicing is known as a *slash chord*, wherein the chord name is indicated to the left of the slash, and the note in the bass is indicated to the right). We've also seen the Dadd4 voicing before but, like the C/G chord, the 5th (A) is played in the bass. Notice that these two voicings are exactly the same; we just need to slide it up two frets when moving from C/G to Dadd4/A.

The Fsus2 chord is a little more challenging to voice, however. The way it's presented here, we need to wrap our thumb over the top of the neck to fret the low F note (fret 1, string 6) while using our other fingers to voice the rest of the chord, including a two-string barre of the index finger. But don't fear! If this chord is difficult to play at first, you can work around it a few different ways: 1) you can let the high E string ring open rather than barre it with the index finger, which also sounds great, 2) you can omit the low F note and just strum strings 5–1, or 3) you can use a combination of these two approaches.

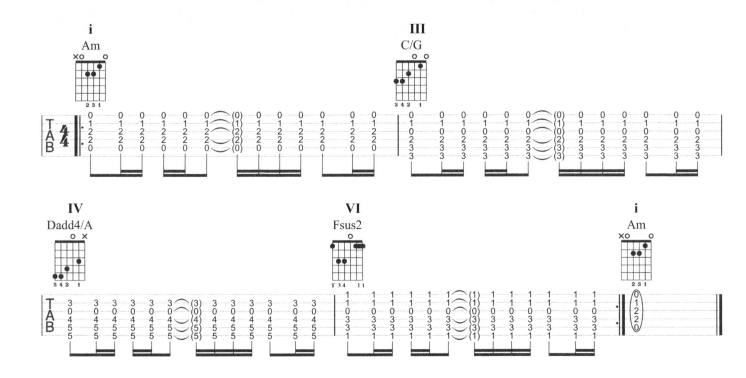

OPEN-CHORD ARPEGGIOS (1:15–1:00)

This arpeggio pattern is pretty straightforward; the only real challenge is the bass movement that takes place in measure 1. Here, the *leading tone* (F#) is used to set up resolution to the root of the G (III) chord. Note how the F# feels unstable, or dissonant, until resolution is achieved on beat 3 (the G chord). This is a great way to create anticipation for various chords in your progression.

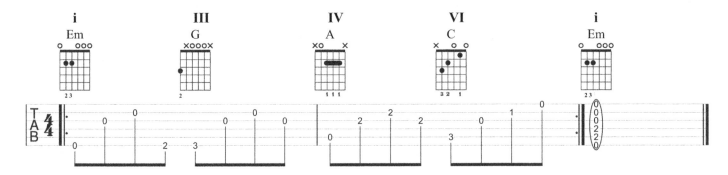

OPEN-CHORD FINGERPICKING (1:00–0:45)

This next example is a little on the longer side but the fingerpicking is a pretty straightforward Travis-picking pattern, so it shouldn't give you too much trouble. The biggest challenge is the bass movement that occurs at the end of every other measure, prior to each chord change.

The majority of the chord changes are comprised of a pinch on beat 1, followed by several alternations of the thumb and index finger. At the end of the F#m and A changes, use your ring finger to grab the G# and C# bass notes that immediately precede the A and B changes, respectively. And use the same technique when moving from the B chord to the D chord. While you're using your ring finger to fret the new bass note for each of these changes, your index finger should remain in place (barred across fret 2) to handle the note the follows on the "and" of beat 4. The D chord is a little different: for this change, keep the D chord voiced and simply pluck the open A string.

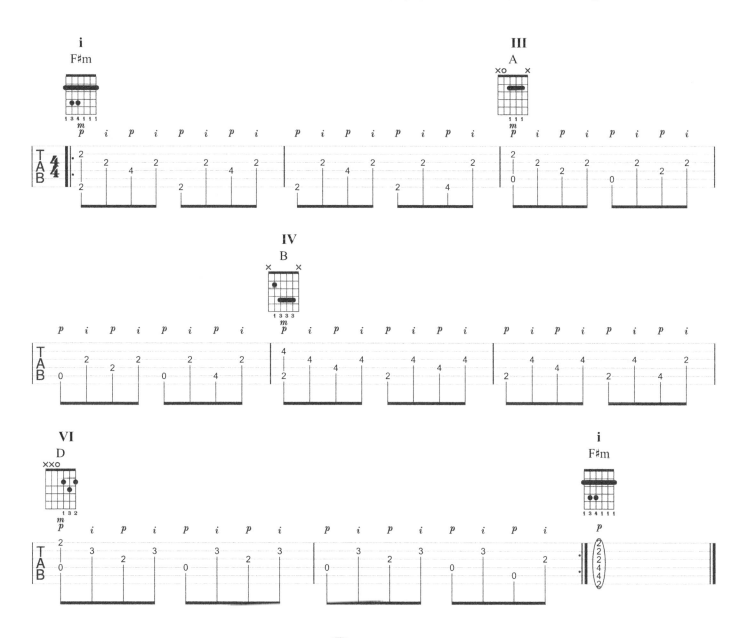

BARRE CHORDS (0:45–0:30)

The i–III–IV–VI progression is handled here with a series of fifth-string-root barre chords that work their way up the fretboard—and create an abundance of energy along the way. Also featured are 16th-note palm mutes that would feel at home in a metal riff.

65

On beat 1 of each measure, strum the dotted eighth not with a downstroke, followed by an upstroke for the 16th note. Then use steady alternate picking for the palm-muted 16th notes. In spite of the additional chord syncopation in measure 4 (Bb chord), use the same approach.

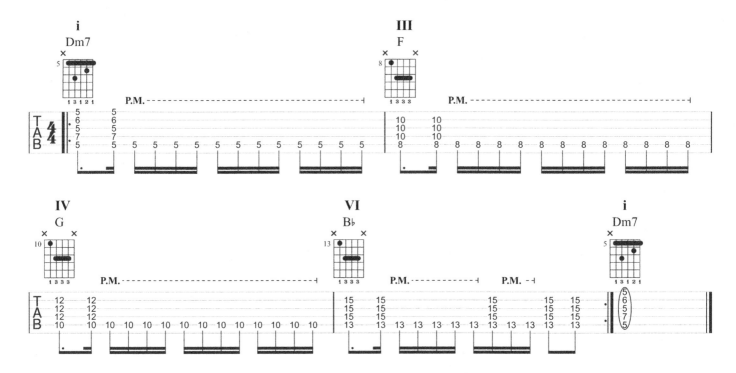

EXTENDED CHORDS (0:30–0:15)

This funky riff features a series of extended chords voiced on the top four strings. To give the progression a little more movement, embellishments are added to string 1. For the Gm7 and C7 chords, simply add your ring finger to the string, two frets above the voicing. Similarly, for the Bbmaj7 and Ebmaj7 chords, add your pinky a couple of frets above the voicing.

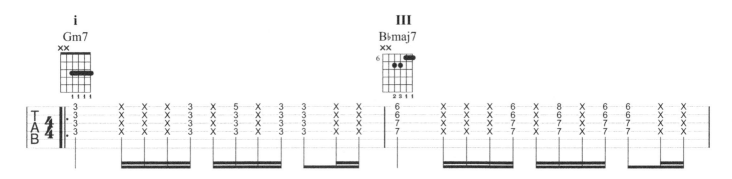

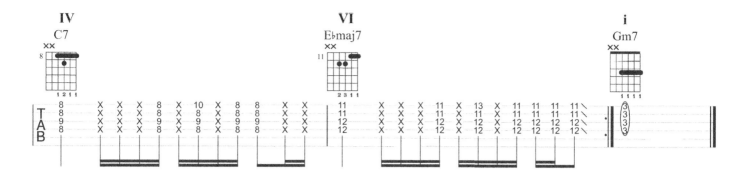

6/8 METER (0:15–0:00)

This 6/8 example is built around a single barre chord (Bm7) and a trio of open chords (D, E, and G). Rhythmically, each measure shifts between straight eighth notes and a syncopated dotted eighth/16th/eighth grouping, except measure 4, where it's all straight eighth notes. Be sure to focus on your picking here because most measures (measure 2 being an exception) require you to skip one or two strings after plucking the root note.

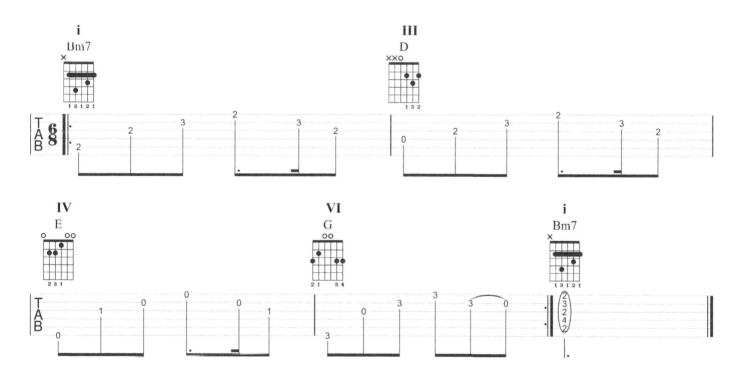

Our second non-diatonic minor progression, i–VII–VI–V7, hit its popularity peak in the '60s and '70s, and even found success well into the '80s. The changes will no doubt sound familiar to you right away due to the string of massive hits to use them throughout the years.

What makes this progression non-diatonic is the use of a major (or dominant) V chord, which is minor in quality in a diatonic minor progression. However, many composers actually prefer the sound of the major V chord in a minor progression due to the presence of the leading tone. For example, in the key of A minor, the leading tone, G#, is the 3rd of the *major* V chord, E (E–G#–B), whereas the *minor* v chord's 3rd is G natural. If you remember, the leading tone has a strong urge to resolve to the i chord—in this case, Am—which is a desirable sound in many compositions. However, the minor v chord, Em, and its minor 3rd chord tone (G), lack this inherent pull, but may still sound great in certain situation.

In this book, we created our minor progressions by harmonizing the *natural* minor scale, which is common and why the i–VII–VI–V7 is considered non-diatonic. But, if we constructed our minor progressions by harmonizing the *harmonic* minor scale, then this progression would be considered diatonic to that scale. It sounds confusing, but the only thing to concern yourself with is the fact that the v chord in minor progressions is often major (or dominant) in quality because it sounds great, even though theoretically it might not be part of the scale being used to construct the song.

EXAMPLES IN POPULAR SONGS:
"A Hazy Shade of Winter" by Simon & Garfunkel (Key of D Minor)
"Good Vibrations" by The Beach Boys (Key of Eb Minor)
"Happy Together" by The Turtles (Key of F# Minor)
"Maneater" by Hall & Oates (Key of B Minor)
"Runaway" by Del Shannon (Key of Bb Minor)
"Stray Cat Strut" by Stray Cats (Key of C Minor)
"Sultans of Swing" by Dire Straits (Key of D Minor)

OPEN-CHORD STRUMMING (1:30–1:15)

This next exercise features a pretty simple strumming pattern that consists of a bunch of eighth notes and a touch of syncopation (on the "and" of beat 2). For both measures, use the following strumming pattern: down-up-down-up-up-down-up. In other words, use alternate picking throughout, except when you reach the tie, where you'll skip a downstroke, and instead use two consecutive upstrokes.

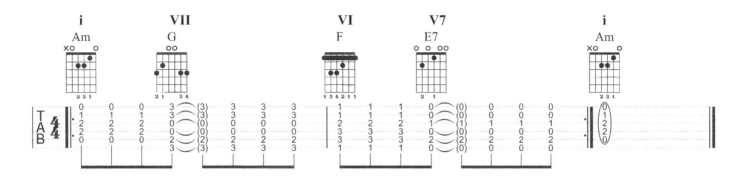

OPEN-CHORD ARPEGGIOS (1:15–1:00)

Here's another pretty straightforward example—at least rhythmically. The challenge here is the harmony, particularly when moving from the VI (Cadd9) chord to the V7 (B7) chord. To make this change, slide your middle and index fingers down one fret on strings 5 and 4, respectively, and then add your ring finger to fret 2 of string 3 and your pinky to fret 2 of string 1. It's the latter move that will prove most difficult, so take it slow at first, increasing your speed incrementally.

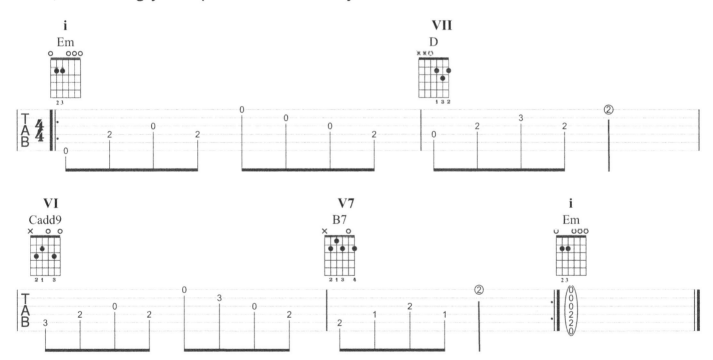

OPEN-CHORD FINGERPICKING (1:00–0:45)

This exercise probably looks harder than it actually is. By now, you should be pretty well accustomed to most—if not all—of the chord voicings used here, and the finger-picking is one, repetitive Travis-picking pattern: *p–i–p–m*. Also working in our favor is the fact that the pattern is confined to the same strings for the F#m and E changes, as well as for the Dadd4 and C#7 chords, so minimal string jumping is required of our pick hand.

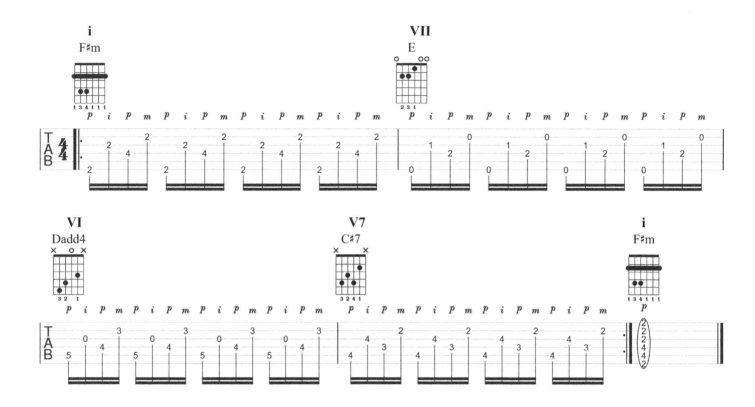

BARRE CHORDS (0:45–0:30)

Six-string barre-chord shapes are used exclusively in this example and paired with scratch chords to create a ska-like rhythm figure that would sound at home in a Sublime song. To cleanly execute the scratch chords, release a bit of pressure from the strings without removing your fingers fully. Then, when you need to sound the chord, simply reapply pressure. This simple muting technique will enable you to place most of your focus on your right hand and getting the rhythm right.

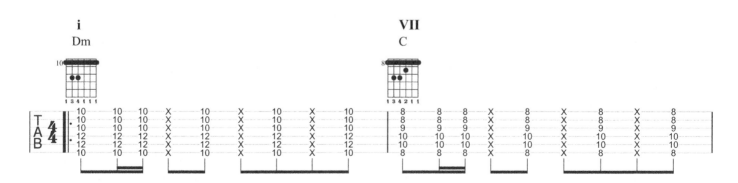

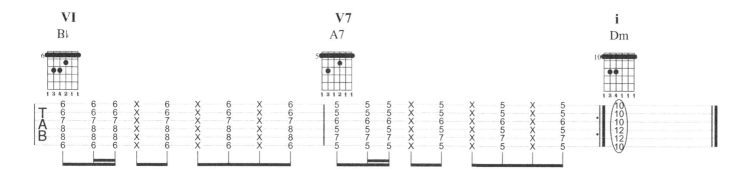

EXTENDED CHORDS (0:30–0:15)

This exercise features five-string barre chords exclusively and works all the way from 10th position to fifth position while cycling through the i–VII–VI–V7 progression. Since all of the shapes require an index finger barre, use this finger as your guide as you move from fret 10 to fret 8 to fret 6 and, finally, to fret 5. Also: be mindful of the rests. We haven't used a lot of rests in previous examples, so it's easy to overlook them. If you have trouble counting them, use the audio demo for help.

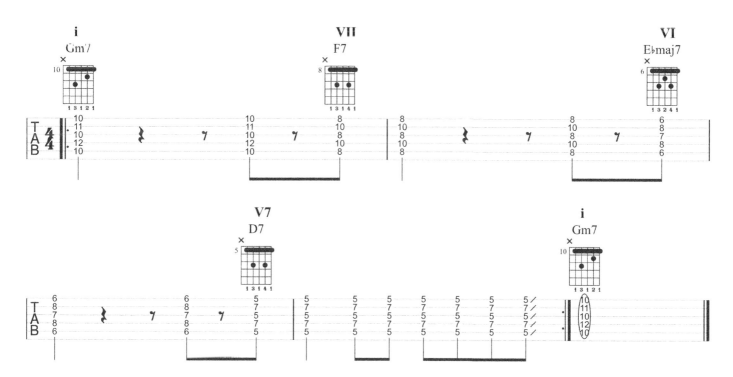

6/8 METER (0:15–0:00)

Our final exercise also gradually works its way down the neck, moving here from seventh position to second position while the chord progression unfolds. The voicings are mostly four-string barre-chord shapes, with the only exception being the F#7 chord (but it, too, is voiced on the top four strings). When you pick this exercise, use one continuous downstroke for the first three notes in each measure, and an upstroke for the quarter notes. Then, for the 16th notes, use a quick down-up combo. Lastly, when voicing the F#7 chord, you'll want to implement an index-finger barre on the top two strings. That way, you won't have to reposition your index finger for the pull-off at the end of the measure.

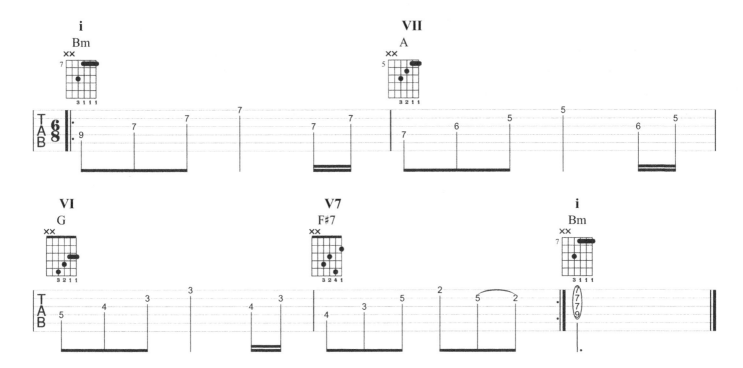

APPENDIX

DIATONIC MAJOR PROGRESSIONS

KEY	I	ii	iii	IV	V	vi	viidim
C MAJOR	C	Dm	Em	F	G	Am	Bdim
G MAJOR	G	Am	Bm	C	D	Em	F#dim
D MAJOR	D	Em	F#m	G	A	Bm	C#dim
A MAJOR	A	Bm	C#m	D	E	F#m	G#dim
E MAJOR	E	F#m	G#m	A	B	C#m	D#dim
B MAJOR	B	C#m	D#m	E	F#	G#m	A#dim
F#/Gb MAJOR	F#/Gb	G#m/Abm	A#m/Bbm	B/Cb	C#/Db	D#m/Ebm	E#dim/Fdim
C#/Db MAJOR	C#/Db	D#m/Ebm	E#m/Fm	F#/Gb	G#/Ab	A#m/Bbm	B#dim/Cdim
Ab MAJOR	Ab	Bbm	Cm	Db	Eb	Fm	Gdim
Eb MAJOR	Eb	Fm	Gm	Ab	Bb	Cm	Ddim
Bb MAJOR	Bb	Cm	Dm	Eb	F	Gm	Adim
F MAJOR	F	Gm	Am	Bb	C	Dm	Edim

DIATONIC MINOR PROGRESSIONS

KEY	i	iidim	III	iv	v	VI	VII
A MINOR	Am	Bdim	C	Dm	Em	F	G
E MINOR	Em	F#dim	G	Am	Bm	C	D
B MINOR	Bm	C#dim	D	Em	F#m	G	A
F# MINOR	F#m	G#dim	A	Bm	C#m	D	E
C# MINOR	C#m	D#dim	E	F#m	G#m	A	B
G# MINOR	G#m	A#dim	B	C#m	D#m	E	F#
D#/Eb MINOR	D#m/Ebm	E#dim/Fdim	F#/Gb	G#m/Abm	A#m/Bbm	B/Cb	C#/Db
A#/Bb MINOR	A#m/Bbm	B#dim/Cdim	C#/Db	D#m/Ebm	E#m/Fm	F#/Gb	G#/Ab
F MINOR	Fm	Gdim	Ab	Bbm	Cm	Db	Eb
C MINOR	Cm	Ddim	Eb	Fm	Gm	Ab	Bb
G MINOR	Gm	Adim	Bb	Cm	Dm	Eb	F
D MINOR	Dm	Edim	F	Gm	Am	Bb	C

Made in the USA
Monee, IL
02 November 2019